Rebecca Front is a BAFTA-winning actress and the author of *Curious*, shortlisted for the National Book Awards, and *Impossible Things Before Breakfast*. She is best known for her work on television, both in comedies such as *The Thick of It*, *Knowing Me, Knowing You with Alan Partridge*, *Nighty Night* and *The Day Today*, and in dramas including *Lewis*, *War and Peace*, *Queers* and *Poldark*. With her brother Jeremy she stars in BBC Radio 4's *Incredible Women*, and she is a frequent panellist on *The News Quiz*. Her columns have appeared in the *Guardian*, *Sunday Times* and many other publications. Born and raised in East London, she read English at St Hugh's College, Oxford, and was the first female president of the Oxford Revue.

Praise for Rebecca Front

'A brilliant storyteller, it's the curious in the quotidian
that attracts her gaze as she spins her funny and poignant
tales'
Scotsman

Impossible Things Before Breakfast

'I was completely captivated by it'
David Sedaris

'Hilarious'
The Times

'Delightful . . . Rebecca Front is an affecting and elegant
writer with a gift for making the ordinary seem extraor-
dinary . . . The book is not only funny but in places
deeply moving'
Sipora Levy, *Jewish Chronicle*

Curious

'Both original and entertaining'
Viv Groskop, *Sunday Express*

'Funny and touching'
Daily Telegraph

'Warm, anxious and true – a little book of uncalm'
Caitlin Moran

IMPOSSIBLE THINGS BEFORE BREAKFAST

ADVENTURES
in the ORDINARY

REBECCA FRONT

WEIDENFELD & NICOLSON

First published in Great Britain in 2018
This paperback edition published in 2019 by Weidenfeld & Nicolson
an imprint of The Orion Publishing Group Ltd
Carmelite House, 50 Victoria Embankment
London EC4Y 0DZ

An Hachette UK Company

1 3 5 7 9 10 8 6 4 2

A CIP catalogue record for this book is
available from the British Library.

ISBN (mass-market paperback) 978 1 78022 612 5
ISBN (audio) 978 1 4096 285 8
ISBN (ebook) 978 0 297 87025 8

Typeset by Input Data Services Ltd, Somerset

Printed and bound in Great Britain by Clays Ltd, Elcograf S.p.A.

For Phil

CONTENTS

WELCOME TO MY WORLD

My father takes a sketchbook with him wherever he goes. Drawing is how he sees the world, how he frames it for himself and fixes it in his memory. The things he draws are tiny, inconsequential snapshots – a child feeding ducks, a woman in a hospital waiting room, the third violinist from the right in an orchestra. If you took a camera and filmed the whole scene, they'd probably be the last things you'd notice. But the act of drawing isolates them from their context and makes them seem much more important than they otherwise would.

When I was little I used to copy him – I always had a notebook and a pencil, and whenever Dad sat down in a quiet corner of a church, say, and started drawing a gargoyle, I'd do the same.

I don't draw any more. But this fascination with detail has stayed with me, at least where people are concerned. I watch people all the time, and I'm an inveterate eavesdropper. I try not to focus on what they're saying, but rather on what they're *not* saying. I'll sneak a peek to find out if their posture or the tension in their hands or their smile belies their words. I thoroughly recommend it. It's the best way to learn about the world – and about yourself.

Sometimes these snapshots draw you into intrigue. A few years ago I was working in St Petersburg, and I went down to the hotel bar before dinner to wait for some of the other actors. I ordered myself a vodka and sat with my iPad in a booth. I hadn't intentionally hidden myself away, but I can't have been all that visible because after a moment or two a couple came and sat at the table right next to mine in the otherwise deserted bar.

The woman was Russian – around twenty, I'd say – and beautiful. Long hair, soulful eyes, a melancholy expression. The man she was with was American – much older, probably in his late fifties. He was pleasant-looking in a kind of crumpled, paunchy way. They sat down and he got them drinks. He didn't ask her what she wanted – just went right ahead and ordered. For a while they didn't talk. Then finally, after the drinks had arrived, he stretched languidly back in his chair and said:

'So . . . tell me a little about yourself, now that we're awake.'

I put the iPad down.

She spoke excellent English, though rather too quietly for my purposes. She was studying something or other at university. Was he her teacher, I wondered? A visiting professor having an illicit fling? He had a much louder voice, thank goodness. He was married – and he talked about his wife a lot. The marriage was stagnating, she didn't understand him. There was a certain amount of *mea culpa* in the way he *said* it, but the subtext was that it was all her fault.

She had 'issues', she was 'needy', things were tough.

That was all I got – my friends arrived and I had to stop eavesdropping and have a conversation of my own. But it stayed with me, that tiny glimpse into the unknown.

Other snapshots can be more mundane.

I bought a coffee at a service station one day, and went to get milk from the table near the counter. In front of me was a man, about sixty-five, tall, thin, grey, wearing the sort of jumper and slacks that were designed not to be noticed. His wife was with him, already sipping her tea while she waited for him to customise his. He took a sachet of sugar, shook it, tapped it on the corner of the table and tore off a strip at the top. But instead of tipping it in, he sprinkled in a few granules, stirred the tea, blew on it, tasted it and sprinkled some more. He repeated this sequence over and over, with the utmost concentration and seemingly no awareness that he was holding up the queue. When he'd finally emptied in the whole sachet, he sipped, thought for a moment, shook his head, and started again on a second one. I glanced at his wife. She had a look of infinite weariness about her, and I realised he must do this every time he had a drink, at home, in a café . . . this was his ritual, his way of controlling what little he could in an unpredictable world.

When I first started writing, I knew that I didn't want it to be about acting. It's not that I don't find that fascinating; it obsesses me for much of the time. But I didn't feel comfortable writing about how I get to grips with a script, or what this famous person or that was like to work with. I wanted to write about the other stuff: everyday life, the details at the edge of the frame. I love little incidents and misunderstandings, embarrassment and confusion. I'm fascinated by our internal monologues – the way we over-think things and worry about stuff when nobody else is aware of us doing so. And the more I wrote about those things, the more I realised that I *was* writing about acting, because in order to play a character, you have to understand them as a person; you have to see them in the round. It's tempting for actors to say 'my character would never do that', but the truth is we don't know what our characters would do any more than we know what we ourselves would do.

People are odd; we do weird things. Even the most pre-dictable of us sometimes defies expectations.

In *Alice Through the Looking Glass*, the White Queen says: 'sometimes I've believed up to six impossible things before breakfast'.

That seems plausible to me – sit on a bus or on a bench in the park, and impossible things will present themselves to you. If they don't, then maybe you need to go somewhere else for breakfast.

I was buying something in a shop recently and got into a conversation with the sales assistant about insurance.

'I've only ever once had to make a claim,' he said, 'but I won't go into it.'

'OK,' I said.

'It was to do with these,' he continued, pointing at his teeth, 'but I won't go into it.'

'Fair enough,' I replied, and smiled to reassure him I wasn't going to pry.

But I'd misread the situation. He was desperate to tell his story; 'I won't go into it' carried with it an implied 'unless you really want me to'. Finally, even without my prompting, into it he went.

'Basically,' he explained, 'my false teeth got eaten by a beagle.'

And there it was, another impossible thing to add to that day's tally. Believe me, the challenge is limiting yourself to six.

Even when there's no one else around, there'll be no shortage of impossible things in your own head – memories, hopes and fears all tossed together like an ill-conceived salad. Often these things pop into our minds and are gone again in an instant. But sometimes they stay a while, link up with other random thoughts and turn themselves into something bigger – an anecdote or an opinion, maybe something as grand as a world view.

Each of us carries around a wealth of stories – the big ones about love and joy and sickness and loss, and the small ones about how we misjudged a situation, about perceived slights and what we should have said in return.

These are the things that make us who we are, the details that create the bigger picture.

The stories that follow are my equivalent to the sketches in my father's notebooks. They're my way of seeing the world, of framing it and fixing it in my memory.

HEAVY BREATHING

Lizzie finished handing out cups of juice to the people gathered in her living room and settled herself down in an armchair.

'So, shall we introduce ourselves again?'

She nodded encouragingly at the woman on her left.

'I'm Cathy and this is my partner, Jonathan.'

Everyone murmured hello.

'I'm Anji and . . .'

'I'm Rav. Anji's husband. Hello.'

We all helloed again.

'Naomi,' said Naomi.

'Steve,' said Steve before adding, 'the guy who put Naomi here!'

Steve was the joker in the group.

'And I'm Rebecca.' They all looked at me, and I could read the pity in their eyes.

'It's just me again. Phil couldn't make it, I'm afraid. Work stuff. You know.'

The fourth week of childbirth classes and Phil had been a no-show every time.

They'd all formed their own opinions of course; I would have done the same. Perhaps the relationship was in trouble, or Phil was married to someone else, or he wasn't really ready to be a father. Whatever their suspicions, they were way too polite to say anything. Except for Steve, that is.

'Blimey. Busy fella, your Phil,' he said, looking around for approval.

'Shut up, Steve,' Naomi hissed, but he was warming to his theme.

'International man of mystery.'

'Steve . . .'

'Is he a spy?'

I smiled to diffuse the tension, even though I wasn't the one who'd created it. But I felt the need to explain. I didn't mind them thinking I was a single mum – there was no stigma attached to that any more. But I didn't want to look like a liar or a fantasist. And the more detail I gave, the more I sounded like both.

'He's in the media,' I said. 'TV and films. So he . . . er . . . he travels a lot . . . LA, that sort of thing –'

Lizzie interrupted me and started the session, which should have been a relief, but actually proved she thought I was making this stuff up.

And I was. Phil wasn't travelling and he wasn't at work. He was, as he had been for the previous three Wednesdays, at home in our flat watching football. Chelsea needed him more than I did, apparently. And even if he wasn't at the match, he still had to perform the vital service of sitting on our sofa screaming instructions at the players.

'Switch it! Switch it! Go WIDE!' he'd be yelling, and

they'd carry on doing whatever they were doing, for all the world as if they couldn't hear him. I'd told him many times that this was why he needed these classes, because if he started shouting 'Go wide' at me when I was in labour, I wouldn't be answerable for the consequences.

But the point is I should have said it was a football night. It would have been simpler and more honest, and maybe they would have sympathised. We'd all have preferred to be watching telly than discussing our perinea with strangers. But I didn't want anyone thinking ill of the man I'd married, dismissing him as immature and sport-obsessed and having NO idea what was about to hit him. I felt that was my job.

'Now this week,' Lizzie began, 'we're going to be looking at the lead-up to labour – the days running up to and beyond your due date. When you start to feel like it's never going to be over, things can get pretty tense.'

There was a ripple of uneasy laughter. The couples grinned at each other in affectionate recognition. I had no one to grin at, so I drew a smiley face in my notebook instead.

'Now there are certain things you can do which may or may not help to get your labour started. Anyone got any ideas?'

Everyone sat there reluctant to speak.

Eventually, Cathy said in a very quiet voice that she'd heard spicy food was supposed to help. Lizzie said she'd heard that too and asked for other suggestions. Another long pause.

It occurred to me that since I was doing the work of two

people here, maybe I should offer up a few. Besides, I've always been a teacher's pet.

'Raspberry leaf tea? Gentle exercise? Driving over speed bumps?' I said.

'Very good,' said Lizzie. 'You *have* been doing your homework.'

I drew another smiley, only bigger this time and wearing a little hat.

'Now you mentioned exercise, Rebecca, and one type of physical activity that a lot of people find helpful is sex.'

There was a cynical groan, as you might expect from a group of heavily pregnant women with swollen ankles and chronic indigestion.

'Of course, that may well be the last thing on your mind at this stage in your pregnancy,' Lizzie acknowledged. 'But any kind of sexual activity produces endorphins and the rush of hormones is thought to be very beneficial.'

The couples looked at each other with differing degrees of anticipation, delight and horror. I looked at my notepad, thinking that if my due date fell on a football night I'd have to rely on raspberry leaf tea and speed bumps.

Suddenly Steve piped up.

'When we say "sexual activity", Lizzie,' he began, and Naomi, who was one step ahead of him, nudged him in the ribs and turned a dangerously hypertensive shade of pink. 'No, I'm just wondering . . .' Steve continued, as if he wasn't asking for himself, but for some sexually frustrated father-to-be friend of his. 'Are we talking only about . . . you know . . . full-on erm . . . actual . . . erm . . .'

'It doesn't have to be full intercourse, no, Steve.' Lizzie was trying to avert disaster before Naomi went into premature labour to spite him. 'Any kind of intimate contact would have the same effect.'

She nodded and smiled, pleased to be the sort of woman who can talk openly about this stuff, and confident she'd cleared up any confusion. But Steve had seen a glimmer of hope on the horizon and carried on hurtling towards it.

'So . . . would it be as effective if it was . . . erm . . . oral . . . erm –'

'God, Steve. Can we drop it now?' Naomi hissed.

'Absolutely, yes,' said Lizzie with a sensible nod, trying to shut him down. 'Whatever takes your fancy. Now, I'm going to pass round an information leaflet about the early stages of labour –'

'Sorry, Lizzie,' said Steve again. 'Sorry to interrupt you. But in the interests of clarity, when you say "oral" . . .'

'YOU said "oral", Steve,' Naomi said. 'Nobody else said "oral". Only you.'

'I just want to be clear. Are we talking about the man . . . erm . . . performing it on the erm . . . Or would it be as beneficial . . . were the woman . . . to erm . . . *give*, er, *go*, er . . . perform it on the er . . .'

Lizzie's smile had faded in the face of such blatant opportunism. With a coldness I hadn't previously seen in her, she said, 'You'd have to do it to Naomi. It won't work the other way round,' and started to hand out her leaflets.

Steve looked crushed.

When I got home that night, I had almost forgiven Phil for not coming to the session. If there was one thing worse than being married to an imaginary husband, I figured, it would be being married to Steve. Still, I wasn't going to let him off the hook too easily.

I sat down in the living room with an audible 'oof'. It was difficult these days to make any kind of move without one. My bag was on my lap and I started to empty out the leaflets Lizzie had given me. Every week I came home with more and more of them. I didn't read them, just piled them up next to the bed, where they stayed like unfinished homework, gathering dust and filling me with silent dread. If Phil had no idea what was about to hit him, then I had enough ideas for both of us. My head was full of complications and pitfalls, birth plans, interventions and emergency Caesareans. I was starting to question the wisdom of these antenatal classes. It was all very well arming yourself with knowledge, but birth was such an uncontrollable thing. Anything could happen, and for all the talk about making choices, I couldn't help feeling that when push came to shove (as it inevitably would), I might be better off reacting to circumstances rather than trying to wrestle them into submission.

'How was it tonight?' Phil said, bringing me a cup of tea.

'OK,' I said, tight-lipped. I wasn't willing to forgive him quite yet. 'Did they win?'

'Nil–nil.'

'Well worth staying home for,' I mumbled.

For a while, I sipped my tea in silence, hoping to convey what a world of pain this goalless draw had put me through. But he dunked his biscuit and hummed a little tune to himself, so I realised I needed to be more explicit.

'I would really like you to come next time, please.'

'OK,' he said.

'OK as in "if Chelsea aren't playing"?' I asked, witheringly.

'No. OK as in "they're not".'

'Oh, fine,' I sniffed. 'So if they were, you still wouldn't come.'

'But they're not.'

'But if they were . . .'

'Bec, where are we going with this? I know you want me to come, and I'm coming.'

'Because you've got nothing better to do.'

'I've got plenty of better things to do, but if you want me to come, I'll come.'

I gave him an incredulous look.

'You've got plenty of better things to do than find out about our baby?'

'That's not what I meant. And neither of us is going to find out anything about *our baby* by sitting around on bean-bags in an antenatal class. So I can't see the point.'

'There aren't any beanbags,' I snapped. 'Well, only a couple. And the point is that we need to be prepared.'

'I think I am prepared,' he said. 'Ask me a question.'

'OK,' I said rising to the challenge. I'd show him how clueless he was about this whole thing.

'What happens if the baby is overdue?'

He sipped his tea thoughtfully.

'Is it like library books? Is there a fine?'

'I'm going to bed,' I snarled.

'Most hospitals will monitor you more frequently once you reach your due date, and if after forty-two weeks there's still no action, they'll suggest inducing labour.'

He did have some idea, then. But I still wasn't satisfied.

'And how would they do that?' I asked.

'Probably using prostaglandin in pessary form. Sometimes more than one dose is needed, in which case they have to leave six hours between them,' he said, smugly.

'You've been reading the leaflets, you bastard!' I shouted.

'You told me to. I thought that's why you left them by the bed. How is that wrong? You told me you wanted me to be better informed.'

'I didn't want you to be better informed than *me*,' I said. 'It's not a bloody competition. I wanted us to learn this stuff together.'

I leapt to my feet – at least in my head that's what I did. But in reality, I turned my upper body slightly sideways, gripped the arm of the sofa and slowly levered myself upwards.

'Goodnight,' I said.

'Bec,' Phil called after me. 'I promise I'll be there next week. And I'll answer all the questions. Or none of them. Whatever makes you happy.'

A week later we were in Lizzie's flat together. There weren't enough chairs for Phil as well, confirming my suspicion that she didn't think he existed, so Phil offered to get one from another room. She told him there was a beanbag in her bedroom and, with a look that said 'of *course* there is', he went off to fetch it. Everybody had settled themselves by the time he returned, so I was irritated to notice that instead of quietly sitting down next to me, he spent some time scrutinising the beanbag, brushing it with his sleeve and blowing on it. Lizzie had noticed it too, and while the other couples were doing their hellos, she kept looking in his direction. Eventually he sank down into it in an ungainly spider-in-the-bath pose, his head on his chest and his arms and legs splayed. I rolled my eyes.

'Now, this week's session,' Lizzie began, 'is on what we call the cascade of intervention. Who can tell me what that is?'

Phil put his hand up immediately, but since he was slumped in the beanbag with his arms already higher than his head, Lizzie didn't notice the difference. I seized the opportunity to score a point.

'I *think* I know . . .' I began tentatively, trying not to sound like the sort of person who'd spent all day revising leaflets so her husband wouldn't be Star Pupil.

'Is it when, as a result of intervening to deal with a complication of labour, further complications arise from that intervention?'

I probably should have loosened up the prose a bit. It sounded suspiciously like I'd learned it by heart, and Phil narrowed his eyes at me.

'That's exactly right, Rebecca,' Lizzie said. I gave a modest shrug, drew a smiley face that covered the entire sheet of my notebook and surreptitiously flashed it in Phil's direction.

'So let me explain what that means,' she continued. 'Let's say that you go into the labour ward, and for some reason the doctors decide to monitor you and your baby. In doing so, you'll be restricted from moving around, and that might make your contractions slow down. So another intervention might be necessary to keep them going. And *that* intervention might in turn . . .'

There was a low, rattling noise coming from my left, and I realised with horror that Phil was snoring. It was quiet now, but I wasn't going to let it get any louder. I turned to jab him in the ribs, but his eyes were wide open, and it became apparent that the position the beanbag had forced him into, with his head pressed on to his chest, was restricting his breathing. Before I could get him to straighten up, Lizzie intervened.

'Now can I borrow one of the dads to do a demonstration, please?' she asked.

Phil volunteered, with what seemed like genuine keenness. He laboriously worked his way out of the beanbag to a standing position, and as he did so, he had a coughing fit. What with that and the laboured breathing, I wondered if he was going down with a cold.

Lizzie asked him to lie down on the carpet, which he did.

'Now you're going to be our pregnant mum,' she said, and everybody chuckled. Everybody except Phil, who was picking something off his T-shirt and looking slightly concerned.

'So, lie flat, Phil,' Lizzie said. 'Sorry about the cat hairs on the carpet . . .'

She got to her feet and began an improvisation in which she – 'the doctor' – attached monitors and IV drips to Phil's 'pregnant mum'. Phil lay passively on the floor, but his chest was rising and falling heavily. I leant forward, as far as my bump would allow, to take a closer look. His eyes were closed, and his brow was furrowed.

I glanced at the beanbag and suddenly realised what he'd been trying to remove from it before he sat down – cat hairs. They were everywhere. I'd never seen a cat at Lizzie's place. Presumably it stayed in the bedroom on the beanbag when classes were going on. But now that I was aware of the hairs, I couldn't miss them. The sofas, cushions and the rug Phil was lying on were covered in them. Phil's allergic to cats. He hadn't been dozing, snoring or coughing all this time. He'd been warding off an asthma attack.

I couldn't understand why he hadn't said anything. And then I remembered how guilty I'd made him feel for not coming. Now that he *was* here, he was trying so hard to participate that he'd put himself at risk. My feckless, good-for-nothing, football-loving, hopeless husband suddenly seemed to me nothing short of heroic.

Either that or he was faking it so he wouldn't have to come again.

I gave him the benefit of the doubt.

'Lizzie, I think Phil's struggling a bit,' I said.

'No, I'm OK,' he said with a breathy kind of rasp.

'He's allergic to cats. He needs to get up,' I said.

Lizzie apologised profusely and helped him to his feet. Since he didn't have an inhaler with him, we both knew there was only one thing for it. I took him down to the car and we got in together and sat with the windows open. After a few moments his breathing settled down again.

'You go back in,' he said. 'I'll be fine now.'

'I'm not leaving you,' I said.

'Really, go back. It wasn't a proper attack – I was just heading towards one.'

'I feel terrible about it,' I said. 'I didn't know she had a cat, honestly. It wasn't some devious plot to kill you.'

'It's fine,' Phil said.

'But you only came here for me. And you volunteered to lie on the floor to impress me. The more you tried to help, the worse things got.'

'Our very own cascade of interventions,' Phil said.

'So you heard all that through the gasping.'

'I knew about it anyway. That leaflet you learned off by heart? I'd learned it too.'

'Well, as long as you're OK,' I said, 'I'll go back in for the last few minutes.'

I walked back up the path and buzzed Lizzie's bell. As I waited, I turned back to check on Phil and he gave me a reassuring wave. He looked better already. The door opened and I went upstairs. Lizzie had opened the window, in case anyone else needed air. With all her experience of pregnant women, she'd clearly never expected a dad-related emergency.

'OK,' she continued, 'now I've got a couple of leaflets about the cascade of interventions. Perhaps you can pass them around.'

From the street outside, I heard a car stereo switch on. A familiar hum of yelling and chanting and a voice saying, 'We're five minutes into the second half here at Villa Park.' And then another voice, muffled, shouting expletives. Actually, 'shouting' is the wrong word – it was more a sort of tired rasp. It was the sound of someone who'd suddenly realised that having a cat allergy carried unintended benefits.

'You've got to hand it to him, he's a smart guy,' said Steve.

'Oh do shut up, Steve,' hissed Naomi.

IMPENETRABLE

It was far too hot to sleep. I'd known that when I went to bed, but I thought if I could just get comfortable and read a couple of pages, then sleep might come. I'd been up since six, I was exhausted. The only part of me still fully functioning was the bit of my brain telling me I'd never get to sleep. I had to block that out. It was a question of not over-thinking.

I lay there trying to concentrate on the words in front of me, blurry as they were in the dim light, but all I could think about was the heat. Ten months of the year, I do nothing but shiver. I walk around the house in a bundling of jumpers, chattering my teeth like some cartoon depiction of a cold person.

But now, on one of the rare nights of the year when the thermometer had nudged above 'balmy', I was hot. Too hot to read. And definitely too hot to sleep.

I threw the duvet off and felt simultaneously cooler and even more awake. So I gave in to the inevitable and sat up. I looked at the clock on my phone: 1.15 a.m. Well, it was early enough. I could get up, read somewhere cooler with a brighter light, come back to bed in an hour or so and still get a good few hours.

Without even thinking, I'd flicked open my Twitter feed. Force of habit. Spooling down, I kept seeing mentions of the Perseids. Tonight was the night for shooting stars, apparently – well, one of the nights. It was a show that happened every year and for several weeks at a time, but tonight with the help of a cloudless August sky it was getting rave reviews on social media.

The Perseids. *That* was the name of it. I suddenly remembered one summer's evening years ago, coming home from a pizza restaurant when the children were small, and spotting a shooting star. Then another and another. We'd sat on a low wall scanning the sky for more, until Tilly began to fall asleep on my lap and we felt that we should be proper parents and take her home to bed. That must have been what we were watching, the Perseids. All those years had passed, and I'd never bothered to look for them again. Odd to have been so star-struck, and then to have forgotten all about it. Well there was no point lying in bed reading what other people thought. I might as well go and see for myself.

I sneaked to the door, grabbing a cardigan in case I ever grew tired of feeling cool air on my skin, which right now I couldn't imagine, and tiptoed down the hall.

Ollie's light was still on. In the summer holidays he operated on teenage-boy time, going to sleep in the early hours, and waking up around noon. I knocked on his door.

'Yup,' he called, so I opened it a little and leant my head around.

'Hot, isn't it?' I said.

'Yup.'

'I couldn't sleep.'

'No. Me neither.'

'Want anything from downstairs?'

'No thanks,' he said. I wasn't expecting much in the way of a conversation – that's why I hadn't gone into the room. Sometimes he was chatty; often you only got a few functional monosyllables. But he never forgot his pleases and thank-yous, and I figured that was good enough. He'd talk when he was ready.

I closed his door and headed off down the stairs. And then a thought occurred to me. I went back up and knocked again.

'Yup?'

'What do you know about the Perseids?' I asked.

'Meteor shower. Shooting stars. We watched it once, coming back from somewhere.'

'I didn't think you'd remember that,' I said.

'I remember everything,' he smiled. It was true, he had the best memory of anyone I'd ever met.

'I thought I might sit in the garden and have a look,' I said.

'Cool,' he said.

'It's got to be cooler than in here, anyway,' I said.

'No, I meant –'

'I know, I know. I was being ... you know ... obtuse. Deliberately. For mildly comic effect.'

He rolled his eyes.

'Well, night then,' I said, and closed his door again.

I was halfway down the stairs when the miracle happened.

'Wait for me, Mum,' he whispered.

*

'So Marge got cross, but Homer didn't know she was cross . . . '

'Oh, OK –'

'And Homer went to Moe's . . .'

'Right. So I suppose that made Marge even crosser –'

'Yeah, then she was *angry . . .*'

Ollie was telling me the entire plot of a *Simpsons* episode on the walk to school. He was probably around eight or nine then; the enthusiastic age. It wasn't always *The Simpsons*. Sometimes it would be the story of a book he was reading, an incident that had happened at a friend's house or a narrative completely invented in his head. The main point was that he wanted to share it – had to, in fact. Because if it had been enjoyable first time around, then surely it could only get better. Right?

Words were Ollie's thing. Talking, walking, reading, writing – children develop them at their own pace, late with one thing, early with another. Ollie had been slow to walk – several months later than all his friends. Partly it was because he had a dazzlingly speedy crawl which got him to most of the places he needed to go, and an obliging mother who'd carry him everywhere else. But mainly it was because he was pouring all his energy into speaking. This was a kid with something to say, and the instant his infant babbling turned into actual, comprehensible words, he was damn well going to say it.

I remember one afternoon around the same time, he'd bought a toy he'd been saving up for for ages. It was a kind of hard plastic sleeve with a disc on top that looked like the Starship *Enterprise*. The idea was that you strapped it to your arm and fed into it a particular brand of trading card that he and all his friends had been collecting. And when you'd fitted the card into the slot at the front of this gadget, you could fire it (the card, that is, not the plastic sleeve, though that would be fun too) right across the room. So you had all the pleasure of buying the cards, reading them, swapping them if you wanted to complete a set, and then watching them fly through space. A complete joy to a small boy and utterly bewildering to anyone else.

The afternoon he bought this card-throwing thing, we sat in a café, just the two of us, and he talked and talked and talked about it. He showed me all the cards, explained why this one was better than that one, filled me in on the stories that went with them, why character A was feuding with character B and so on. And finally, when I'd paid the bill and we were walking through the rush-hour bustle to get home, he talked about the best rooms in our house for card-throwing. The kitchen was long, so the card would fly further, but his bedroom held the added challenge of bunk beds. Would a card fired from the floor make it as far as his top bunk? It was clearly a thrilling possibility.

It didn't actually work, the throwy thing. Those kind of gadgets rarely did. He tried it as soon as we walked in the house, and the first card got snarled up in the mechanism, while subsequent ones lolloped bathetically on to the carpet by his feet. But it didn't matter. Well it did, but not for long. Because for him, the anticipation was everything, and for me, it was all about hearing him talk.

A few years passed and we sat in the same café at the same table where he'd told me every detail about those cards, but this time in silence. He was at secondary school now and a year or so into the boil and swirl of growing up: desperate to blend in, eaten up with self-consciousness, wondering who to be today. Teenagers are torn between two contradictory beliefs – that they're the centre of the universe and that life isn't all about them. Deep down, it was obvious Ollie was every bit as enthusiastic about stuff as ever – he just wasn't sure it was OK to show it. And so we sat, stirring our hot chocolate and looking out of the window. I asked him questions and he answered them with as little information as he could politely get away with. It was all heartbreakingly predictable, and I understood that it had to happen for the sake of society. We can't go through our lives thinking everything we say is so important that the whole world needs to hear it. But of course for me, Ollie's mother, he *was* the centre of the universe. Life *was* all about him. I didn't care what he talked about as long as he was talking to me. Those impenetrable childish monologues were infinitely better than this impenetrable silence.

I learned to wait. To sit patiently and wait. Because if the old Ollie was still in there – the enthusiast, the teller of tales, the describer of details – he'd emerge from time to time, like a flash of light across the night sky. I just had to be there to see it.

It didn't last long, the taciturn phase. He figured out pretty quickly that not talking enough was much more boring than talking too much. And as he learned more about the world, having a conversation with him no longer relied on your knowledge of a cartoon series or the relative merits of Top Trump cards. Now we could talk about friends and sport and current affairs. A dry-as-dust sense of humour began to emerge, replacing the uncontrollable giggles he'd had as a child. Here was the grown-up version of our Ollie starting to find his voice, trying it out on us first, over the dinner table and from the safe seclusion of the back of the car, before opening it up to the unpredictable responses of a universe full of strangers.

Ollie put out two garden chairs facing the same direction. The sky was all around us, of course, and stars could shoot from anywhere to anywhere, but I think in his head he was picturing a kind of astral drive-in movie. So I sat down next to him and we both tilted our faces to the heavens.

I don't know what I expected – a light show, fireworks, the aurora borealis – but there wasn't much to see. Nothing happened. We sat and waited and our eyes slowly adjusted to the darkness and began to pick out more detail, a few more stars, a little more sparkle. From time to time one of us whispered something to the other. He told me stuff about meteor showers; I asked him questions or shared with him random thoughts that popped into my head. But mostly we sat in silence, a companionable silence that we felt no need to break.

Suddenly we saw it: a vivid streak of silver that passed directly above our heads, but so fast I almost thought I'd imagined it.

'Did you see it?' Ollie hissed.

'Yeah. Amazing,' I whispered back.

We sat for a few more minutes, trying to guess where the next one might appear. Once or twice we got excited over a satellite or the tail lights of a plane. But then we settled back in our seats and carried on watching for another small miracle to occur. I wrapped my cardigan around me. I seemed to have bypassed pleasantly cool and gone straight from too hot to too cold. But I didn't want to go inside. Not yet.

The more I stared into space the deeper into the void my eye was drawn. What had looked at first like a murky black sky now revealed more and more tiny pinpricks of light. There they all were, as they always had been and always would be. The darkness wasn't impenetrable after all. It was filled with light; you just had to take the time to look for it.

I moved in my chair to see a different part of the sky and it scraped noisily on the patio. Ollie shifted his gaze down to me.

'You're not going in, are you?' he asked. And the faint hint of disappointment in his voice was a shooting star piercing my heart.

He wanted me there. I wasn't an irrelevance, an irritation. He wasn't humouring me. I was as big a part of this experience for him as he was for me. We needed each other as much as we needed the night and the stars and the anticipation.

'No, I'm not going in,' I whispered, suppressing a shiver. 'I wouldn't miss this for the world.'

We stayed out there for an hour, maybe more. A few more stars flew by. Not many, but it didn't really matter. Even as we marvelled that the world wasn't all about us, we still felt like the centre of the universe.

There will, I know, be moments in the future as dark and huge and impenetrable as that night's sky when I first looked up at it. And to get me through those moments when they come, I'll try to remember what it felt like to sit side by side with this man – my boy – in the chill summer air. Watching and listening, talking and being; gazing at stars and waiting for them to dance for us.

SHOWING MY TEETH

There was a monster in our town, and they called him Driller. When you're a child and you believe in such things, your one consolation is that your parents will keep you safe. But no – here we were, my brother and me, waiting to be taken into his lair, and it was our own mother who'd brought us there. Jeremy was eleven and clearly not thrilled about this; I was seven and flat-out terrified.

I don't suppose anybody wants to be at the dentist, do they? Possibly not even the dentists themselves. I mean, what the hell kind of a job is that, peering into people's mouths all day, scraping off plaque and making their gums bleed? I'm not belittling it – it's vital work and someone's got to do it. But at what point in childhood, faced with life's endless possibilities, do you think: 'Actually, I'll skip being an astronaut or a train driver and do root canals on people with halitosis instead'?

Anyway, this particular dentist – Mr Bulmoor – was a paediatric specialist with the chairside manner of a torturer.

Nobody knew why he was so unpleasant. Mum thought maybe he'd been unlucky in love. Dad suspected money worries. Jeremy reckoned Bulmoor simply hated children. Then why specialise in paediatrics, we all asked? Jeremy said that was the point – if you *really* hated kids, what better revenge could there be than performing dentistry on them? Perhaps he was right, or perhaps, as was more likely, there'd been a staff meeting at the practice, straws had been produced and Bulmoor had drawn the short one. In that moment, a glittering future of crowns and porcelain veneers had turned instead into the daily grind of fixing sweet-induced tooth decay. Whatever lay at the root of it all, Bulmoor's signature style was gung-ho and interventionist, his unspoken motto: 'Drill it, fill it or yank it out.'

My dental health, up to that point, had been excellent, thank you for asking, so there was no real reason for me to be terrified of dentists, except that I was scared of everything. But when my mother first told me about the appointment, I flatly refused to go.

Now the notion of a seven-year-old refusing to go somewhere might strike you as odd; it might, indeed, meet with your disapproval. So perhaps I should take the time at this point – as Driller might have done – to fill in a gap or two.

I'm the youngest in the family by several years. This gave me one great advantage – I was able to watch what Jeremy did, how he navigated his way through life, and learn from his mistakes. He, like many elder children, was even-tempered and amenable. And if Mum and Dad found him less than eager to, say, go to bed early or eat his greens, then they had a few simple tricks up their sleeves. They'd promise him an extra story at bedtime or some ice cream the next day, and it almost always worked. Four years down the line, when I was refusing to go to bed or eat my greens, I'd had a chance to witness all of this. I knew what their negotiating strategies were, and was one step ahead all the time.

I saw the same dynamic at work with my own children years later. If Ollie complained at bedtime, we'd say, 'Go up now and you can have an extra chapter of *Harry Potter*.' But when we tried the same thing on Tilly, she'd tell us she'd rather skip the story and stay up late, and we'd have to come up with a whole new strategy.

So for my mum, who'd never had to deal with anything worse than a frown and a jutting lip when Jeremy didn't want to go somewhere, my flat-out refusal was uncharted water. My mother was in fact a teacher, and an impressive one at that. She could control a class of forty boys without breaking a sweat. But my stubbornness baffled her. Nobody else in the family was quite as intransigent as I was. If I decided I didn't want to do something, there wasn't much – short of brute force, which my parents were far too liberal to use – that could make me do it.

In order to get me to the dentist's that day, Mum had had to resort to the one tactic that never failed – bribery.

There was, at the time, a type of collectable doll that I coveted. They were called Liddle Kiddles, and each one represented a flower – a rose or a violet, a bluebell or a lily of the valley; her hair and dress were red, purple, blue or green accordingly. And here was the clincher, they all lived inside their own little plastic bottle which, when opened, exuded a sickly chemical approximation of that flower's perfume. I'd been saving up my pocket and birthday money for weeks to buy these dolls and now only needed Lily of the Valley to complete the set. Mum promised that if I went to the dentist she would buy me the doll.

I'm sensing that disapproval again, so let me just say that anyone who tells you they never use bribery on their kids is lying. But there are rules, the most important of which is never to give away the bribe until after the child has done the thing you're bribing them to do. This is where things went awry for my mother.

In order to get to the dentist by bus, we had to pass the toyshop, and since Dad was giving us a lift home later, Mum's only chance to buy the doll was on the way there. She did so surreptitiously and hid it away in her bag without my noticing. But the closer we got to the dentist's, the more hysterical I became, and because I needed comforting and she needed a quiet life she handed over the doll.

Now, as I sat in the waiting room, clutching the tiny green bottle with its gaudy, smelly doll inside, we both knew I held all the cards. Of course I'd *try* to be a brave girl while Driller did whatever Driller needed to do, but ultimately if I couldn't go through with it – well, you know, whatever. I still had my doll.

The waiting room had jaunty educational posters on the walls, one of which was a before-and-after cartoon of a rabbit. In the first he looked sad, with a handkerchief wrapped around his jaw. In the second he was happily chomping a carrot and winking. The caption read: 'There's nothing BUNNY in tooth decay. Why not HOP to the dentist today?' But even sophisticated wordplay couldn't distract me from the raised voices and bursts of drilling wafting through the closed surgery door.

After a while, the door opened and a dental assistant appeared, ushering out a boy of around Jeremy's age walking stiffly and sniffing. Like the cartoon rabbit, he had a handkerchief clutched to his mouth, only this one was covered in blood. The nurse led him over to his father, saying in a quiet, regretful voice:

'Mr Bulmoor had to extract them both.'

'Extract?' said the father. 'We thought maybe a filling or two . . .'

'I'm sorry,' she said, and gave a kind of helpless shrug which could have meant 'there was nothing else to be done', but read more like 'my boss is a bit of a bastard'.

The man smoothed his son's hair down over his red, puffy face, put a steadying arm around him and led him away.

All three of us had watched this scene unfold, and Mum and Jeremy braced themselves for what was about to come.

'Rebecca Front next, please,' the nurse called across the waiting room.

Mum stood up but I stayed in my chair. She took my hand firmly, but I wouldn't budge.

'I'm coming in with you,' she said, but I'd started to sob. The tears were genuine, although I do remember noticing that the waiting room acoustic nicely enhanced my wailing.

'I'll wait here,' Jeremy said, and I couldn't really blame him.

'Come along now,' said the nurse, and she tried to grab my other hand, the one that was clutching my doll. I pulled it away from her in case she tried to take it hostage.

I firmly believed I could stay in the waiting room through sheer force of personality. But there was one crucial thing that I'd misjudged. I was tiny enough to be picked up and carried, and with no bribe left and an absence of other ideas, that's what Mum now did. She transported me efficiently through the surgery door, and on to the monstrous-looking black leather chair. Then she nodded curtly to the nurse, who shut the door and stood in front of it.

I stopped crying out of shock, and it took me a moment to grasp what had happened. While I tried to make sense of it all, I looked around. Everything about this room was alien and terrifying. The chair was like no chair I'd ever seen before. It wasn't comfy like the ones at home or utilitarian like the ones at school. It was vast, shiny and slippery, like some huge, child-eating beetle. The lights weren't like normal lights either. They were big and round and searingly bright, and had spindly arms attached to them, all the better to reach you with. Everywhere I looked, there were other unfamiliar things, and, since I had no way of identifying what they were for, they remained just *things*, things on stands and things on hooks, things that were sharp and spiky and things that had rubber hoses coming out of them. The whole place smelled clean, but not in a good way.

In my silent horror, I looked at the doll for reassurance, but her sweet smile now looked like a grimace. Before she'd seemed cosy inside her bottle, now she was as frightened and trapped as me.

The door opened, nearly knocking over the dental nurse who'd been guarding it, and in walked Mr Bulmoor. He was tall and pear-shaped – although that might have been the cut of his surgical coat – and he had the sort of face you knew you wouldn't remember if you ever saw it again. He was leafing through a buff-coloured folder and didn't look up from it, even when Mum said hello to him in a slightly ingratiating 'don't hurt my child' kind of way. For what seemed like an eternity he leant against the sink reading and Mum carried on gamely smiling in the hope that he'd turn into a human. Finally he mumbled, 'Germy?'

Mum glanced at the nurse, who frowned and looked nervous.

'Sorry, Mr Bulmoor?' she said.

Driller looked up from the folder and stared at the nurse.

'Is it germy?' he said.

The nurse looked puzzled.

'I don't think ... I'm not quite sure what ... I mean, everything's been autoclaved, if that's what –'

'Jeremy!' Mum suddenly blurted.

'Yes,' said Driller, still staring at the nurse. 'What did you think I meant?'

'Jeremy is my son,' Mum explained. 'But he's not here. Well he is, but he's in the waiting room. This is my daughter.'

And with that, for the first time, Driller turned his icy stare towards me.

'Name?' he asked, sizing me up as if calculating whether my tiny frame might make me cheaper to anaesthetise.

Mum told him my name and date of birth. Then, in case he hadn't already guessed it from the way I was wriggling in the chair, she added, 'She's a bit nervous.'

He walked towards me menacingly, peered at me over his glasses, reached up with one arm and yanked the adjustable lamp so that it was shining right in my eyes. I instinctively turned my head away, and he barked, 'Head still, little girl.'

I screwed my eyes closed and clutched my doll.

'Open,' Driller commanded.

I opened my eyes.

'Mouth,' he corrected, and I felt like an idiot.

The nurse scuttled towards him and handed him a long metal wand, with a tiny mirror on the end, which he unceremoniously shoved on to my tongue.

I could feel my eyes welling up. I wanted to cry, but my mouth was gaping, so all I could do was grunt.

Driller then produced a spiky stick and started prodding my teeth, all the while murmuring things to the nurse in code, like 'lateral incisor, cuspid, cavity'. None of it meant anything to me, but it didn't sound encouraging. Finally he withdrew both the spike and the mirror and barked, 'Rinse.'

I looked at Mum and she gestured towards some sickly pink liquid in a glass by the sink. I picked it up, sniffed it and put it back down.

'You're supposed to gargle with it,' Mum whispered. But I shook my head so vehemently that she mouthed, 'Doesn't matter.'

She turned towards Mr Bulmoor and gave him that nervous smile again.

'So what's the verdict?' she asked.

He was scribbling things in his folder and declined to look up.

'Three fillings,' he said.

'Three?' said Mum. 'Is that absolutely necessary?'

Driller stopped writing and slowly raised his eyes towards her.

'Do you have dental training, Mrs Font?' he asked, with faux politeness.

'Front,' Mum corrected. 'And no. Only I thought, what with them being milk teeth . . .'

'I recognised they were milk teeth, Mrs Font,' he said in a voice of chilling calm. 'We covered that on day one of dental school.'

'Yes. Of course. But . . . she doesn't seem to be in any pain . . .'

'Oh well then, let's leave it,' snapped Driller. 'Might as well wait until she is. We wouldn't want your daughter to miss out on suffering any pain, would we?'

'I . . . obviously don't want that. I meant . . .'

'Three fillings,' Driller growled. 'Take it or leave it.'

I knew Mum well enough to know that she'd never ignore an expert. There was only one thing for it. I had to take control. OK, I was little, but these were my teeth, and that was my mum he'd been rude to. And besides . . . I already had my doll.

I wriggled my way out from under the lamp, shimmied down the chair until I got past the weird sink with the pink drink on it and clambered on to the floor.

'What do you think you're doing?' demanded the dentist.

I replied with a presence of mind that came from I knew not where:

'I think you'd better see my brother now.'

As I legged it to the door, I could hear Driller shouting, 'You're a very silly little girl!' I turned briefly and caught sight of Mum, her face frozen in a rictus of apology. She looked helpless, trapped and slightly green, exactly like the Lily of the Valley doll.

Of course, I see now that I should have run away without offering up my brother as a sacrifice. I don't think Jeremy has ever quite forgiven me, but as I often say to him, that molar might have needed extracting anyway.

What strikes me most when I remember that story though is how very different the adult me is from the little girl. Somewhere along the line I lost that gutsy determination, that stubbornness, that willingness to take action. I also lost my fear of dentists, so it's not all bad news. But now, in my middle years, as I look back at that tiny creature, I realise that though I was frequently scared, I was never timid. I knew what I wanted and what I didn't want. And I wasn't prepared to put up with unreasonable behaviour.

When I ran from the dentist that day, it was a positive act, not a negative one. I wasn't running away, I was taking a stand. Somehow, in turning into a grown-up, I stopped doing that and started going along with things instead.

An older friend once told me that the great joy of ageing is that she no longer gives a shit what people think of her. I haven't got there yet. I still worry too much about seeming polite and being liked. But up until now I've been using my energy elsewhere – learning to face my fears. Now that I've made such progress with that, I think there's a new challenge ahead. I have to rediscover how to be bold, how to confront, how to speak my mind.

I need to start showing my teeth again.

BY THE SEA

One blazing-hot Saturday afternoon on a beach on the west coast of the USA, a mother and daughter sat down on the sand. The spot they happened to choose was right in front of where I was sitting. Now if you don't want your every move watched and your every word eavesdropped on, you probably shouldn't come and sit near me. Certainly not when I've been in one place for too long and am starting to get bored. I may appear to be reading my book or playing a game on my phone, but in fact I'll be listening to you.

The mother had on a light skirt and a straw hat, the daughter a pink sundress and brightly coloured beads. As she set to work building sandcastles, her mum took photos and fetched buckets of seawater. It was all quietly idyllic. But not for long. Moments later, into the frame strolled a bearded man fully dressed for the office in a short-sleeved, stay-pressed shirt, long trousers, socks and street shoes. He was carrying a folded-up camping chair and, as he arrived, the woman turned, smiled at him and pointed to where she thought he ought to put it.

He lifted his sunglasses on top of his head and scrutin-ised the suggested patch of sand, smoothing it over this way and that with his foot. He curled his lip disapprovingly and shook his head. Then slowly he unfolded the chair in a different spot. It was just a few feet away from and identical in all respects to the one his wife had recommended, except that he had chosen it himself. He made sure the chair was fully open by rattling the metal arms, pressing down hard on the canvas and checking it would take his weight, and finally settled himself into it. His wife and child watched this ritual from the corners of their eyes, and only once it was completed did they carry on building sandcastles.

For a long time the man gazed silently at the horizon.

Eventually, in a gloomy monotone, he spoke:

'You guys know what to do if the water gets sucked out, right?'

The mother and child smiled at him, resignedly. They'd known this question was coming.

'You run like hell,' said the father in response to himself, 'cos that's the first sign of a tsunami.' There was a pause, during which his daughter patted more claggy sand on to her castle, and the sea rolled benignly on the way it was meant to.

'A lotta people see that happen,' he resumed, 'and they stand there and watch. Think it's kinda cool, the sea draw-ing back like that. Well . . . they're the ones that don't make it.'

The woman stood up and walked a few yards to pick up a shell. She brought it back to the girl, who placed it carefully on top of the castle.

'One time,' the man continued, with a morbid laugh, 'I

read it in the newspaper, this ten-year-old kid said to her parents, "When the ocean does that, doesn't it mean a big wave's coming?" Ten years old. She knew right away something wasn't right. Good job too, or they wouldn't have made it outta there.' A pause and another bitter laugh. 'Ten years old. Knew more than all the rest of them put together.'

His own little girl, no more than six, ran down to the water's edge to refill her bucket. In the circumstances, it looked like an act of rebellion. But her dad said nothing and irritably brushed sand from his shoe.

Further down the beach someone waded into the sea for a swim.

'Sure hope he knows what he's doing,' the bearded guy murmured. 'This time of year, when it's hot, a lotta people think the water's gonna be warm. But it isn't. Not here. Stay in too long and . . . boom. Hypothermia. Your heart can give out. Just like that. Goodnight, Vienna.'

His wife took a surreptitious snap of him. I wondered if she'd put it on Facebook with the caption 'We had a great day at the beach'. Then she slipped off her shoes and gazed at the treacherous sea, envious perhaps of its ability to kill without remorse.

'Another thing people don't know: currents. They see these little waves? Oh, they look safe enough. But you get a current going this way meets another going that way, and even a strong swimmer can't fight that. They start out here, next thing they're halfway to Alaska. No way back. (Pause) Yup. They never tell you that in surf school.'

I lifted up my sunglasses to get a better look at him. Maybe that's where this unhappiness stemmed from; perhaps he'd been sent to surf school by his parents against his will. I could imagine him, summer after summer, a tiny middle-aged child, sitting on his towel on the sand, refusing to engage with the rip tides and the stingrays and the sharks, and scoffing as the other kids put themselves in peril.

He reached into a side pocket attached to the chair, pulled out a flask, unscrewed the lid and took a long drink.

'Ah. That's good. And you know what? It's free too. Did you see those people back there, waiting in line at the juice bar? Craaazy. What are they charging? Four, maybe five dollars for a little plastic cup? No wonder people get dehydrated. Take one look at those prices and they walk right out again. In this heat. And that's an expensive mistake to make, my friend, cos if you don't drink on a day like this then you are in for a whole world of trouble.'

He took another swig from the flask, while his wife and daughter thirstily watched him.

'Dehydration. The silent killer.'

And with a weary sigh, he put the flask back into its canvas pocket, and the whole family gazed out to sea in silence.

I thought he might have exhausted himself, but he soon began again.

'What do you want to bet there's jellyfish in there? That'd be the icing on the cake, wouldn't it? If you don't get frozen to death or dragged out to God knows where, you get a sting as big as your head. Man, that's gonna hurt.'

His wife smiled faintly and nodded, and to spread some cheer, she handed her daughter a biscuit.

'Make sure the gulls don't get that, sweetheart,' said her dad, with lightning speed. 'They'll swoop down and take it clean out of your hand, if you don't watch out. I've seen it happen. Kid sitting just like you eating a piece of cake. Bam. Gull got it. Nearly took his fingers too. Last time he made that mistake.'

The girl wrapped up the biscuit and put it back in her mum's bag. She looked around her nervously. The woman put an arm around her shoulders and kissed her head. Then she slowly began to pack their things away. He'd won.

The day trip was over. Only one thing had got sucked away from the beach that day, and it wasn't the sea – it was joy.

If you were asked, in a hypnotherapy session, say, to think of a happy place, a place of tranquillity and beauty where everything felt right with the world, then many of us would conjure up a beach. The glinting azure sea and endless expanse of sand we've all seen in holiday brochures. A beach is a pervasive, persuasive image. All the elements rolled into one – earth, water, fresh air and the fiery sun. An escape from the everyday, a removal from stress. So we save our money, book our holiday and buy a piece of a dream. But from the moment we arrive, correct me if I'm wrong, all we want to do is make this magical place a bit less . . . beachy.

Going to the seaside as a child was always a triumph of hope over experience. As we made the sandwiches and packed the car, we all believed this was going to be the best day ever. Everybody else believed it too, which is why we'd hit traffic as soon as we got on the dual carriageway. The two-hour journey would stretch into three. We'd run into a service station, desperate for a wee, and suddenly remember why having your swimsuit on under your shorts wasn't a time-saving measure after all.

By the time we arrived the tide would be out, but we'd put our towels down on the boggy sand and shiver, while Dad wrestled with an ineffectual plastic windbreak. Mum would open the sandwiches – squashed and warm and gritty with sand the minute you picked one up. In the gaps between running along in pursuit of the flying windbreak, we'd sit and imagine what the sea would have looked like if we'd come a few hours earlier when the tide was in. And on the way home we'd talk about how much fun we'd had – and mean it too – but deep down we'd be thinking we might have had more if the sea had been closer and warmer and the sand hadn't chafed our thighs; if we'd had more shade and not got sunburned.

I remember those days out with real affection, though it may not sound like it. And when I grew up, got married and had children of my own we began taking them on beach holidays too.

With a little more disposable income, we could afford to go to Italy rather than Southend. And for years we went to the same beach, beside the Ionian Sea in the parched, gnarled south of the country. On the surface at least it was more like the ones in a holiday brochure. The sea was as calm and clear as blue glass, and there were quiet coves and dunes and even rock pools if you went looking for them. But Italians like their beaches *managed* on an industrial scale, and Lido Meraviglioso was no exception.

The first time we visited it and saw its row upon row of matching sunbeds and parasols with barely enough space to move between them, I honestly didn't think I'd last a day. So many people, so much noise, too hot, too close, too intimate. But we'd been driving around all morning looking for a place that felt safe for the children – not too rocky, not too deep, not too exposed to the sun – and here the sea was shallow and warm, the sand was clean and you could pay for shade, so I stuck it out for their sakes – I know, I know, I'm self-denial personified. After a while, I began to warm to the fact that there were toilets and you could get cold drinks and snacks and ice creams. The children loved the swings in the car park and spending their pocket money on grabber machines in the mini-arcade next to the bar. There was even a pretty good fish restaurant only yards away from the sunbeds. We fell in love with the soft sand and the bath-water sea too, but what we really loved was everything about this beach that made it more like being in a town.

You could even shop here, and sometimes we did – not merely for the fun of doing so barefoot and in our underwear, but also because we felt guilty. As we lay on a sunbed enjoying our wealthy, white privilege, a steady stream of migrant Thais and North Africans hawked up and down in the crippling heat bearing vast, unwieldy burdens of towels, sundresses and novelty dirigibles. From time to time they'd take a break and sit exhausted on the edge of an unoccupied lounger. They'd mop their brows, flex their aching shoulders and stare out to sea. And I'd wonder what they made of it all – of the casual inequality, the incomprehensible weirdness of a world where black people still do the heavy lifting while white people put all their energy into trying not to look so white.

And so the days turned into a week here and a fortnight there, and we began to come year after year after year. And here's the brilliant part: all the other families on the beach did the same. So even though we barely exchanged more than a '*buongiorno*' or a smile as we passed by on our way to get an ice cream, we felt as though we knew them. As is my way, I'd lie on my sunbed pretending to read and watch them: imagining their lives away from this place; seeing how their kids were growing; trying to guess – since, to my shame, my Italian has never improved since the first time we came – what they might be talking about.

I didn't bother with the English. There was no mystery there. I could understand their conversations, and judge them by what they were reading. It was all too easy. They were essentially the same as us.

Years of British beach holidays have taken the same toll on my fellow Brits as they have on me. We always carry extra layers, because you can't rely on it not to get chilly, and rainwear because you can't rely on it to stay dry. We wear huge straw hats so the pesky foreign sun can't burn us to a crisp. And our men favour capacious, knee-length shorts, suitable in any weather, which somehow, however jaunty the pattern, will never attract attention.

Italians, by contrast, are at ease. They trust their climate to deliver. And as testament to this confidence, Italian men favour an altogether briefer type of swimwear.

Nothing brings out the prissy, E. M. Forster, English maiden aunt in me like being in the presence of skimpy swimming trunks. They leave so very little to the imagination that you have to wonder why you'd bother putting them on at all. As Italian men return from the sea, brushing past you reclining on your sunbed, they have to squeeze through the narrow lanes between the rows, their pelvic regions unavoidably at face-height. You cannot help but learn the size, positioning and circumcisional status of each passer-by. You might wonder why I don't look away, but being prissy is not the same as being incurious, and anyway wherever I turned there'd be the same view. They're garishly coloured, these scraps of lycra – they draw the eye. Like a peacock fanning its tail feathers, this is all about display. So even from a distance, you can't help but notice whose members have become shrunken from the sea, and whose engorged by proximity to other scantily clad bathers.

In spite of these eye-popping distractions – and let's be honest, on occasion because of them – we seemed to be closing in on our ideal beach experience. Yet in those early years, when the children were small, the days followed a fraught routine.

Phil is not remotely as anxious as me, and with his *carpe diem* attitude to life he's as far from Miserable Beach Guy as it's possible to imagine. But in his own way, he too likes to control his environment. I hesitate to call him a control *freak* since I consistently benefit from his planning, booking and arranging, and if I carp about it then (God forbid) I might have to do it myself.

But right from that very first day on Lido Meraviglioso, while the kids were paddling and I was spying on the neighbours, Phil was working out how we could make our holiday run more efficiently. He was hoping, in other words, to wrestle the beach into submission.

He learned very quickly that the best sunbeds – the ones closest to the sea and the bar – were pre-booked by the Italian families who had been coming for years. If you didn't get to the beach before all the other suckers who hadn't reserved, you'd be shoved into the windy corner near the loos, with the acrid smell of frying calamari pumping out of the restaurant kitchen air vent. So every day of our holiday, with the children still under ten, he would wake us up early, bundle us into the car and hare along perilous white roads towards the sea – a man on a mission.

Now we had the view of the sea we wanted. There was just that pesky sand to deal with. So Phil turned his attention to that. At least an hour before waking the rest of us, he'd be up preparing the beach bags with military exactitude. There is, it turns out, a right way and a wrong way to pack one, and if you, like me, thought that it was simply a question of putting in a towel, a book and some suncream, then you have a good deal to learn, my friend. Firstly, everything from the previous day has to be meticulously de-sanded. You may think that this is a pointless waste of time since it will all be covered in the stuff within seconds of arrival, but you'd be wrong. I can't quite remember what Phil's reason was, but I'm sure it was a good one and made a lot of sense. Secondly, changes of clothes must be provided IN A SEP-ARATE BAG. This is to avoid their being contaminated with sand before the end of the day, even though they *will* be the very second you remove them from their hermetically sealed unit and put them on your grease-smeared, grit-encrusted skin. Again, there was a perfectly sound reason for this, but I forgot it the moment I was told it, and some-how couldn't summon up the interest to ask again. Thus we would arrive at the beach every morning of the holidays bleary of eye and foul of temper, schlepping luggage that a Sherpa would baulk at. At least we weren't next to the toilets . . . so I had to concede he was right about that. But that didn't mean we could relax for the day. Oh no.

Because Phil's system made perfect sense to him and absolutely none to the rest of us, we couldn't help but get it wrong. It was based, like the governance of some medieval city state, on a network of legislation so complex that it was only understood by the person who'd created it. Every time we tried to get something out of a bag we'd mistakenly open the One That Must Remain Sealed or fail to do up the zip of the other one properly or leave something lying in the sun that ought to have been in the shade. Phil was a TV producer at the time. His daily life was taken up with fore-seeing problems and working out the minute details that make a project run smoothly. Our vacation had become an extension of his work. Instead of *enjoying* a beach holiday, he was *producing* one.

As the children grew old enough to look after their own stuff at the beach, things took a turn for the better. Even more so once Phil announced triumphantly that he had cracked the arcane '*prenotazione*' system, and had managed to pre-book our sunbeds the way the Italian regulars did. No more early starts, no more wheel-spin drives through tiny village streets. We could take it easy, have a leisurely breakfast before we set off.

We'd turn up when we fancied it, each of us carrying our own bags, some of them partially unzipped as if no harm could possibly come from a speck of sand getting inside. It felt . . . well, as if we were on holiday.

But the glory days were short-lived. The vacuum left by his departing anxiety was simply filled by mine. And now that I was in charge of worrying, we moved on from the sand being our natural enemy; it was the sun that threatened us instead. The new order worked thus: I'd nag the children to put on suncream. They'd half-heartedly do so. But it was never good enough. I wanted to see them smeared like Channel swimmers head to toe in Factor 50. I'd repeat government health warnings about melanoma and they, with slightly worse grace than before, would put on a little more. I'd then scrutinise the positions of everybody's sunbeds and move them around the tiny patch of sand we'd hired for the day until everyone was completely shaded, even if they had to lie uncomfortably close to each other and with one leg tucked under a towel. They'd agree to stay in exactly that configuration on the understanding that I would shut up. I'd remind them that sun damage is a silent killer; that even if it didn't give them cancer, it would wither them like raisins before they were thirty. I'd further point out that I was only acting this way out of a mother's natural solicitude. I'd ask for an apology and be unhappy with the tone of the one I got. And finally I'd get bored by the sound of my own voice and storm off for a walk to calm down.

When we look back on these beach holidays, we only remember the good times – of which there were many. But our competing anxieties drove us and each other crazy. When you're on holiday, you've got time for your resentment to breed. We go away to clear our heads. But once we've done that, what do we think is going to fill the void?

For someone who is self-aware for a living, it took me a surprisingly long time to figure out why the reality of beach holidays always fell so short of the promise. Indeed, I don't know that I would have recognised it at all had it not been for Miserable Beach Guy. For all my amusement at his endless stream of negativity, there was something unsettling about him. It wasn't just that he was imposing all this gloom on his wife and child – though that was awful to see. No, it was that I kind of agreed with him. There was nothing in his whole grim monologue that I could call ridiculous, save for the fact that he'd said it out loud.

Beaches are idyllic – I'm sure they are. They *are* like the pictures in the brochures, like the 'happy place' we all imagine. But then we turn up and ruin them. We bring our stress and our irritation and our desire to control with us, and mess it all up as surely as our footprints mess up the sand. Miserable Beach Guy was right about the rip tides and the risks of dehydration. My dad was right about needing a windbreak. Phil was right about keeping the clean clothes free from sand and I was right about the dangers of sun damage. But we were all missing the very thing we'd gone to the beach for in the first place. We were missing the softness of the sand and the coolness of the wind and the glorious heat of the sun. We were missing the awesome power of the sea too. Or rather we were seeing it and trying to manage it, all the while knowing – like Canute – that we never could, that it could devastate us in an instant and that that was what was so amazing about it.

We go to the beach to get close to nature, but our own nature – the human kind – keeps on getting in the way. We carry our neuroses around with us like those exhausted, weighed-down towel-sellers at Lido Meraviglioso. And after months and months of doing this at work and at home, it's no wonder we yearn for a happy place where we think we'll finally relax. But that beach we're picturing, that happy place – it only exists in our absence. We'll never get to enjoy the holy trinity of sun, sea and sand. What we'll see instead is an unholy oblong – sun, sea, sand and us. So even if a beach is nirvana, it can't be while we're there, *because* . . . we're there. Spoiling the view.

POSITIVE AFFIRMATION

I was walking around a large department store in Barcelona one morning when I realised I was doing that thing again. Instead of heading in a straight line towards whatever I was looking for, I kept getting out of other people's way. I seem to spend half my life stepping aside, weaving around, giving way. Somewhere inside me is the sense that everyone else takes priority over me, that their journey is more important than mine, that I'm stopping them going about the vital business of being them, simply by being me.

My children have called me out on it since they were small. They would wonder why everybody else seemed to walk in straighter lines than we did; why their friends' mummies didn't keep ducking into doorways and apologising. And even though I'm aware of it, I've still never mastered the confident, purposeful stride. It's just not who I am.

But that morning, I started to wonder if perhaps it could be.

Self-help manuals frequently talk about positive affirmations. The theory goes that people like me (and possibly you) hamper our lives by continually retelling a negative story about ourselves: 'I'm not important, I'm not successful, I don't deserve to be listened to . . . ' – that sort of thing. The good news, however, is that we can rewrite that story by saying positive things: 'I'm just as important as everyone else, I can be successful, I deserve to be listened to . . .' Now my problem with all this is that I find self-help books incredibly irritating. While they undoubtedly work for a lot of people, I've yet to get through more than a chapter of one of them without hurling it across the room and yelling, 'What a load of bollocks!' Of course it's very appealing to believe that one can improve one's lot through the simple act of thinking upbeat thoughts, but such a belief carries with it the worrying corollary that everything bad is therefore somehow your own fault. Lost your job? Home been repossessed? Got cancer? Maybe you just weren't peppy enough. Perhaps I should take the potential good and ignore the implicit bad, but I'd rather have no truck with any of it.

But there in that store far from home, weaving around aimlessly as if conveying my lack of self-confidence through the medium of dance, I decided to give it a try.

I stood up straight, pushed back my shoulders and strode towards a mirror. Glancing at my reflection, I realised I looked pretty normal – almost bland if I was going to be self-critical. But since I wasn't, I'd stick with 'normal'. OK, I thought, I'll start from there. Here we go. Let's try this affirmation for size:

MOST PEOPLE DON'T KNOW I'M WEIRD.

It wasn't exactly life-enhancing, but it felt quietly encouraging. I stepped away from the mirror and repeated it in my head a few more times as I moved around the coat section.

MOST PEOPLE DON'T KNOW I'M WEIRD.

The more I repeated it, the more I knew something wasn't right. Of course it wasn't upbeat enough, but that wasn't the issue. I was, after all, only dipping a toe into the supposedly healing waters of positivity, so I couldn't expect to unearth a can-do fountain. But it was more than that. In fact, there were three troubling assumptions in that one statement: firstly that I'm weird, secondly that that's a bad thing and thirdly that the only bright side to my *being* weird was that most people may not have spotted it.

It needed some finessing, that was clear. But first I needed to steer myself out of the way of some purposeful shoppers and briefly dodge into the ladies' loo because an assistant had looked at me oddly. That done, I felt able to put my mind to a second draft. This is what I came up with:

MOST PEOPLE DON'T THINK I'M WEIRD.

This seemed to me to glide smoothly over the issue of whether or not I am in fact weird and whether or not it would be a bad thing if I were. It rested instead on the comforting assumption that most of the people I encounter in my daily life don't consider me weird, or at least don't take a view on my weirdness – whether it exists or not. Strangely – and perhaps as evidence that I *am*, in fact, quite weird – I found this affirmation comforting. It gave me a little spring in my step to think that people weren't judging me as harshly as I judge myself.

I'd left the shop by now and was standing at a pedestrian crossing. It was a busy road, and the noise of the traffic gave me the confidence to do what every self-help book I've ever glanced at tells you to do – to try my affirmation out loud and see how it would feel to release it into the air.

I took a deep breath and said, with all the upbeat, self-confidence I could muster: 'MOST PEOPLE DON'T THINK I'M WEIRD.'

But the roar of traffic which had emboldened me had also concealed the fact that a woman was now standing next to me at the crossing. She shot me a look and swiftly began to cross the road even though the pedestrian light was red.

I'd been right all along – positive affirmations were definitely not for me.

I was in Barcelona to shoot a film, and frankly I was quite surprised to find myself there. By that I don't mean that I'd intended to go to Valencia; that I'd been so busy getting out of people's way that I'd accidentally got on the wrong plane. No, I mean that when the part in the film first came up I had no intention of taking it.

My agent rang me on a very crackly line and told me there was a script on its way. Normally I'd be told lots of other stuff, like who was directing it, where it was being shot and which part I was being considered for, but the line was breaking up so badly that the only audible words were 'film', 'script' and 'read'.

When it arrived, the covering email didn't enlighten me either, my agent having assumed I'd heard all the information over the phone. So I opened the script and started to go through it, hoping it would become obvious what part I should be looking at.

There were, somewhat unusually, three female characters

over the age of thirty-five. The first was described as 'tall, willowy and effortlessly chic'. I desperately wanted it to be that one, but thought it unlikely. The second was 'a blue-stocking academic filled with quiet despair' – that seemed more like it. And the third was the villain of the piece – 'a she-mountain' who, 'filled doorframes with her monstrous bulk'. She would loom up behind people and kill them in implausible ways. As a 5' 4" woman of medium build, I was confident that wouldn't be me.

Actors are always asked in interviews what persuaded them to do this or that project, and since you're not sup-posed to mention the fact that you have a mortgage to pay and your kids can't wear the same pair of shoes year in and year out, we focus instead on 'the challenge the character presents' and 'the quality of the writing'. Now it's quite true that writing is at the heart of any project. If the script's no good, then it's very, very hard to make a good film and it's very, very hard for an actor not to be rubbish in it. But if we were all being totally honest, most actors would admit that the first thing we do when we're sent a script is count the lines. Before we even begin to get to grips with the story or the style of dialogue, we scroll through the document mum-bling to ourselves, 'Nothing in that scene . . . nothing in that scene . . . three lines in that scene', and so on. It's not that you can't be good in a small part, but it's harder to make an impact. And you need to know the job will be worth leaving your family, giving up your social life, traipsing through sta-tions and airports and sitting around for days on end in a draughty little trailer for. It's about art, undoubtedly, but it's also about pride, status, enjoyment and, yes, money.

So, since this is not an interview, I can admit that I was

scrolling through the film script counting the number of times Bluestocking Academic would get to demonstrate her quiet despair, when an email popped in from my agent.

'I thought it might help if you knew who was already cast,' it began, and went on to list the parts that had gone to other actors. The list included 'Effortlessly Chic', as I knew it would, but also, bewilderingly, 'Bluestocking Academic'. I was mystified. That could only mean one thing – that the part they wanted me to consider was the massive, hulking, brutalising woman-mountain. This was either terrifically exciting or frankly bloody ridiculous, and having explored the entirety of that spectrum in my mind I emailed my agent and said it wasn't for me.

But the movie wouldn't go away. I protested that they'd clearly sent it to the wrong person, that I was totally wrong for the part, that nothing in my CV of satirical comedies and historical dramas could possibly have led to me being cast as a woman who could prop up a burning roof with one hand while dispatching a muscle-bound young actor with the other. But the message that came back was 'the director wants to discuss it with you'.

Now there's an old theatrical joke which is a particular favourite of mine: An actor comes home one day to find his house is on fire. His neighbour is in the street and the actor asks him what happened.

'I don't know,' the neighbour replies. 'Apparently your agent was here and he smelled smoke. He called the fire brigade. But don't worry, your wife and kids are safe.' There's a pause, while the actor tries to process all this information. Finally he says: 'So let me get this straight. My *agent* was at my *house?*'

The sentence 'the director wants to discuss it with you' falls into the same category as 'your agent came to the house'. It's a rare occurrence, and even if it doesn't lead to anything great, it's still something you can brag about to other actors. So I agreed to a Skype call that evening and went upstairs to wash my hair and put on some make-up. I was determined to look as glamorous as possible – firstly in a peevish, self-defeating attempt to prove I was wrong for the part, and secondly because there might be some other part in the future – maybe an effortlessly chic one – that he might consider me right for once he'd seen the error of his ways.

The Skype call lasted about half an hour. When I got off the phone, I went into the kitchen and put the kettle on.

'Well?' Phil asked.

'I think I'll give it a go,' I said.

'Blimey, he must be good-looking.'

I gave that comment the disdainful look it deserved, and told him how Ramón (the director) had simply explained to me – in his charming Spanish accent – that he never envisaged the character looking the way she was described on the page; how he'd been both disarmingly modest and boyishly self-effacing and what a great sense of humour he had, considering his prodigious talent.

'So, really good-looking, then?' Phil said.

'Really good-looking,' I confessed.

On my first morning in Barcelona I had make-up and costume checks. I'd put some make-up on myself in the wee small hours before my crack-of-dawn flight – a bit of mascara, eyeliner and some judicious concealer. Helen, the make-up designer, apologised for what she was about to do, then removed every trace of what I was wearing, bushed up my eyebrows with a pencil, gave me the faintest trace of a moustache and said, 'There we are. You're done.' I'm used to it – I didn't become an actress for the glamour. Which is just as well really because next I was taken to the wardrobe department. There were racks and racks of diaphanous blouses and elegantly bias-cut dresses. Not one of them was for me. It was obvious which was my rack – the sea of beige and mushroom. A-line skirts, shapeless cardigans, old-fashioned, orthopaedically approved shoes. It was all true to the director's vision – he wanted my character not to be the terrifying monster described in the script, but to be ordinary, nondescript, the sort of woman you wouldn't either notice or remember. Not until she crept up behind you and knocked you flat, that is, and indeed, probably not then either.

But making me look ordinary was the easy bit – making me look like a killer would be more of a challenge.

I was taken down to a basement room, somewhat ominously lined with crash mats. Think padded cell and you won't be far off. After a brief wait, the door opened and in walked a young actor of around twenty – tall and powerfully built. He introduced himself as Ed, and we both realised that this was to be the first of my 'victims'. I stood to shake his hand and he towered over me, which made us both laugh at the ridiculousness of this whole enterprise. Nobody in their wildest imagination would give me a chance against him in a fight. Nobody, that is, but Ramón the director and his secret weapon, stunt co-ordinator Pep, both of whom now entered the padded cell.

Ramón greeted me and Ed and, since this was the first time he'd seen me in the flesh, I fully expected him to real-ise at last what a terrible piece of miscasting this was. It's a mark of how cussed I can be that, even though I'd commit-ted to doing this movie and was now rather excited at the prospect, I would still have welcomed the director sending me home, merely because it would prove me right. But in-stead he pulled up a chair and told us how he imagined our fight would be filmed.

'The thing about your character,' he said to me, 'is that she doesn't have time for this silly kid. He gets in her way, he's gonna be killed. End of story.'

'But how?' I asked. 'I mean, there's quite a lot more of him than there is of me.'

'Of course,' Ramón said. 'That's the point of movies. In real life it couldn't happen – that's why we pretend.'

I couldn't argue with his logic and nor did I want to. I'd signed a contract and come to Barcelona. My job now was to be whoever he needed me to be – and if that was a ruth-less, cold-hearted killing machine, then fine, why not? I'd give it my best shot.

Ramón moved his chair into the far corner of the room and handed over to Pep.

Now, even though I'd never played a part like this before, I have worked with stunt and fight co-ordinators several times, and the one thing you can guarantee is that they'll always make you feel worse about things before they make you feel better. Their job is not only to make the scene look good on screen but also to ensure that nobody gets hurt in the process. They conduct thorough risk assessments and have a duty to run through those risks with everyone involved. Which is absolutely right and proper, of course, but a nightmare for someone as risk-averse as me. So as Pep talked to us about anodyne stuff like warming up our muscles to avoid injury, all I could imagine was me in one of those full-body casts you see in cartoons. When he explained that a punch to the face would, in reality, be a punch *very close* to the face, I kept thinking how easy it would be to misjudge that and break Ed's nose.

By the time he suggested trying out some fight moves, I was terrified and wishing I'd never agreed to this. But I had, and it was too late to back out. So I parked Scared-of-Everything Rebecca and replaced her with School-Swot Rebecca – the one who listens to every instruction and carries it out to the letter in order to get top marks.

'OK,' Pep said, 'first of all, Ed's going to run at you. I need you to head-butt him, then put your hands on his chest and push him across the room.'

We walked it through slowly to begin with. Ed moved towards me as if he was going to attack me. When he was within striking range, Pep told me to grab Ed by the shoulders, then move one hand to the back of his head and appear to pull his hair. I copied exactly what Pep told me to do. I wouldn't actually *pull* Ed's hair – I would simply rest my clenched fist on top of his head and he would jerk his head back *as if* I was pulling his hair. The same went for the head-butt – all I had to do was move my head towards Ed's, and as long as we timed it properly and made the right noises it would look as if we'd made contact. We did the move in slow motion. It felt ridiculous, but we definitely weren't in any danger. So we tried it quicker, and repeated it again and again until we felt ready for a full-speed run at it.

Ramón took out his phone and began filming to see how it would look on camera.

Ed and I went to our respective sides of the room, grinned at each other and mouthed a very out-of-character 'good luck'.

Pep counted us in.

'Three, two, one – action!'

Ed rushed towards me, I gave a kind of world-weary shrug as if I didn't have time for all this, then grabbed him by the shoulders, fake pulled his hair, head-butted the air about three inches to the right of his head and pushed him away with virtually no pressure at all, but enough of a grunt to sound as if I was hurling him off me. Ed was doing 90 per cent of the actual work, throwing himself around and sliding down crash mats. For me, it was simply choreography with a bit of acting thrown in.

As soon as we'd finished the sequence, Pep came over to each of us and checked we hadn't pulled any muscles or accidentally clumped each other. Then Ramón called us over to watch the video.

It was, we were amazed to see, completely believable. Pep's ingenuity, combined with total commitment from me and Ed had made the impossible seem horribly plausible. Not only was my David taking on Goliath, it looked like Goliath didn't stand a chance.

'And that,' Ramón said, 'is before we add in different camera angles and sound effects and blood, and then edit it all together. So you see what I mean about the power of movies? We've turned you into a killer.'

All this had taken place the day before my weaving-around

-the-shop experience. Now, as I walked back to my hotel, I ran through it all in my head and felt a thrill of pride. And for the first time, a thought occurred to me. If I could come across on camera as a ruthless, kick-ass, fighting machine by virtue of a little make-believe, then why couldn't I act my way into being more confident in everyday life? Maybe this was my version of a positive affirmation; instead of expecting a statement to change my story, I could simply use what I do every day of my working life – I could ACT more confident.

I straightened my spine, pushed back my shoulders and lengthened my gait. I strode purposefully and confidently the last few yards towards the hotel. It felt great.

The hotel had a revolving door, and as I stepped in, a woman rushed into a separate section of it coming the other way. I didn't want to hold her up – she looked like she had somewhere important to go. So I tried to push the door faster, but in doing so I stubbed my toe, brought the door to an abrupt halt and bumped my nose on the glass. The woman looked back at me and shook her head in bafflement.

'MOST PEOPLE DON'T THINK I'M WEIRD,' I whispered to myself.

BATTLING THE ELEMENTS

I was lying on the front-room carpet watching Saturday-morning telly when Mum told me we were going outside.

Normally she'd have said 'we're going out', or named the place we were going to, so I looked up at her, slightly puzzled. But I could see she was agitated.

'Come on,' she added, with a marked increase in urgency.

'Where are we going?' I asked.

'Outside,' she said again. 'Just outside. You won't need your coat.' She had a faraway, anguished look, as if some distant horror was approaching.

'Shall I put the telly off? Will we be long?'

'No, leave it, Bec, we're only going outside,' she said a third time, as if that somehow made things clearer.

'But why?' I asked.

'Because your father's about to put the kettle on.'

When I was growing up, feminism was still a niche interest. Women had the vote, of course, and the Pill, they wore jeans and had jobs and were more independent than at any other time in history. But the prevailing view, at least in our North-East London suburb, was that certain norms were not to be tampered with. The wife did most of the childcare, the husband earned most of the money. The wife drove the car to the shops, the husband drove it on motorways. The wife cooked and sewed and the husband did DIY.

In a tiny way, my family was already bucking that trend. Dad worked at home while Mum taught in a local school. Sometimes he was the breadwinner, but sometimes she was. They both cooked and if you wanted a button sewn on, it was Dad you'd ask, not Mum. Definitely not Mum. She often told me one of the happiest days of her life – right up there with graduating and getting married and having children – was when she discovered iron-on school uniform name labels. So by the standards of all the other families we knew, Mum and Dad were years ahead of the feminist curve. But there were limits. And one of the few areas where my father's sense of gender-appropriateness was unwavering was that of DIY. Decorating, replacing washers on taps, changing light bulbs – these were a man's job. You only had to look at TV or glance at a magazine to see that. Blokes, *real* men, had toolkits and workbenches and probably a shed, and they knew how to use them. They'd slip on a pair of overalls and have the job done in no time, bish bash bosh. And the 'little lady'? 'Her indoors'? She'd love you for it. That's not the way Dad would have put it, you understand. But deep down, he couldn't quite shake the conviction that fixing things was the way to a woman's heart.

In reality, Dad was already firmly entrenched in Mum's heart. She loved the fact that he could (though not all at the same time) drive on a busy motorway, knock up a stir-fry and draw an on-the-spot free-hand representation of the fan-vaulting in York Minster which would draw gasps from passing tourists. She loved him, in short, for being the man he was, doing the things he was good at. There was, and remains to this day, no bigger fan of my dad's talents than my mum. She didn't need him trying to impress her. The need, on that score, came from him.

Maybe creosoting a fence met some atavistic need to protect his family from invaders. But more likely he resented paying another man (and it always was a man, back then) to come and do something he could have a stab at himself.

There was one additional factor in all this. Mum's father (Bampa, as we kids called him) was a builder – self-taught and very successful. This was a man who could create whole edifices from scratch. If the DIY movement had wanted a poster boy, they would have picked Bampa. In my memory, I always picture him bent over the bonnet of our car, glasses on his head, a fag dangling from his lips, refusing to be defeated by something as basic as an engine. Bampa was an all-rounder – he could do wiring and plumbing, he could mix cement, hang doors and lay flooring. Indeed, so utterly confident was he of his DIY skills that on one occasion – and if you're of a squeamish disposition I suggest you skip the rest of this paragraph – when a doctor had suggested the removal of a cyst on his neck, he'd got hold of a sharp knife and a bottle of TCP and decided to do *that* himself too.

Not only was Bampa an eminently, and almost exclusively, practical man, but he couldn't conceive of the notion that every other man wouldn't be the same. So he'd given my father sets of tools, drills, ladders, workbenches and cursory instructions on how to do this job or the other, certain that Dad would find it as easy as he did.

This was, and I mean no disrespect to Dad when I say it, like giving a toddler a Kalashnikov.

The first few jobs he undertook were pretty straightforward, and he saw them through diligently and successfully. He changed a couple of fuses, drilled the odd hole, hung a picture or two without a hitch. All of which dangerously increased his self-confidence. Pretty soon, he started to think he could save himself a tidy amount of money if he had a go at other stuff too.

One weekend, while Mum was hoovering the front room, there was a screeching noise from the vacuum cleaner, quickly followed by a powerful smell of burning rubber. Then it stopped working altogether. Dad put it down on its side and tried to see if some foreign object had wedged itself in the bottom, but since there was nothing immediately apparent, Mum suggested he should take it to the repair shop the next day, and that's what he agreed to do.

But in the morning, once Mum was at work, Dad had second thoughts. How difficult could it be, he wondered, to unscrew the plate at the bottom and see what was going on inside? And if it turned out that a coin or a marble had worked its way in, then he could save himself the wasted time and money of a trip to the shop.

He removed the plate and looked closer, but he couldn't see anything. Then, since he had gone this far, it seemed silly not to go further. He began removing parts – a screw here, a brush there. As he got deeper into the mechanism, a warning voice in his head told him that it might prove tricky putting it back together again. So, playing to his strengths, he grabbed a pencil and a sheet of paper and began to draw a chart of which bits came from where – how the knee bone connected to the thigh bone, if you like. This obviously slowed the process down a bit as, being an artist, he didn't want to do a substandard representation of anything, even if it was only a part of a Hoover that nobody but he was going to see. So for each part he unscrewed, he drew a perspectively accurate sketch, cross-hatched to indicate where the light source created a shadow. Then he numbered it, to indicate the order in which it should be replaced. He passed a couple of hours in this way, humming, I like to imagine, a contented tune, until he suddenly realised that Mum would be coming home for lunch soon. Mindful of the fact that he was *supposed* to have taken it to the repairers, and that in trying to fix it himself he had also failed to complete any of the actual paid work he should have been doing that morning, he started to rush things to a conclusion. Working backwards through his impeccably illustrated notes, he reassembled the Hoover, plugged it in, realised to his disappointment that simply taking it apart had done nothing to fix it, and managed to bundle it into the boot of the car before Mum walked through the door.

'Did you take the Hoover in?' was her first question.

'Oh yeah,' he said vaguely. 'I thought I'd run it up there this afternoon.'

And so he did, explaining to the repairman what had happened when Mum had been using it the day before but carefully omitting the part about him dismantling it.

The next morning, the phone rang. It was the man from the repair shop.

'Mr Front, I wonder if you could help solve a mystery,' he began.

Dad broke into a cold sweat. 'I'll do my best,' he said, trying to sound casual.

'Has anybody been tampering with it at all? Children perhaps? Or . . . anyone else?'

Dad was usually truthful to a fault, but there was manly pride at stake here.

'Erm . . . no. Don't think so. It just stopped working.'

'Right,' said the voice on the phone, with what sounded very much like a smirk. 'Well . . . the surprising thing is how it could ever have worked at all. I've been in this game a long time' – he was warming to his theme now, probably showing off to his colleagues – 'and I can honestly say I've never seen one put together in the way yours is. It's quite a miracle of engineering.'

'Is it?' said Dad, sheepishly.

'It is. Well, it *was*. I'm afraid we've reassembled it somewhat. It's more . . . shall we say, conventional now . . . but you should find it cleans your carpets better.'

He never admitted it to the repair-shop owner, but Dad did eventually own up about the Hoover to Mum. The seeds of doubt about his DIY abilities were sown that day.

And the ground was more than fertile.

To say that Mum is a worrier doesn't begin to cover it. She's spent a large proportion of her life anticipating disaster. Let's say Dad had gone round the corner to post a letter and got waylaid chatting to a neighbour. Mum would instantly assume that he'd fallen, hit his head on a paving slab and was lying unconscious in a pool of blood. So from the moment he told her he'd tried and failed to rebuild an electrical appliance without any expertise whatsoever, she knew he couldn't be trusted not to try the same stupid stunt again.

Jeremy and I thought this was rather unfair. After all, he'd only made the one mistake. And he was an intelligent man – he'd know from now on when he was out of his depth. If he said he could fix a thing, he probably could.

So when the hot water stopped working one Saturday some months later, and Mum went on and on to Dad about getting in a plumber and NOT TRYING TO FIX IT HIMSELF, we backed him up and told her she was over-reacting. Mum and I were due to go into London that day to buy somebody a birthday present. Initially she refused to go, fearing that Dad wasn't taking her seriously. But eventually, nagged into it by me and reassured by the fact that Jeremy – who was then a sensible fourteen-year-old – was going to keep an eye on Dad, she caved in. We went up to town and spent a happy hour or so shopping. Just after lunch, Mum said she was going to find a call box and see whether the plumber had been.

Jeremy answered the phone. He sounded strained.

'Everything all right?' Mum asked.

'Yes,' he said. 'I think so. The fire brigade have left now, but there's still a lot of mopping-up to do . . .'

It turned out that her worst fears had been realised. The minute we'd left the house, Dad had swept Jeremy along on a tide of derring-do. He was sure this little problem was fixable. After all, plumbers charged a fortune – especially at weekends and in an emergency. And how difficult could it be to sort out . . . whatever it was that needed sorting?

According to Jeremy, somehow in the darkness of the loft, balancing precariously on one of Bampa's ladders, holding a torch in one hand and a monkey wrench (again, Bampa's) in the other, Dad had accidentally snapped off and lost in the water tank the crucial part (I don't pretend to know what it's called) that would stop it overflowing. He had tried vainly to retrieve it, but with the water level rising inexorably in the tank, he'd begun to panic that maybe this job was going to be harder than he'd foreseen.

Jeremy had run the gamut of emotions from hysterical laughter to all-out fear before finally persuading Dad to dial 999.

I grew up, therefore, seeing both sides of this stand-off. Dad was right to say he wasn't an idiot; Mum was right to say he sometimes behaved like one. Dad was right that Mum tended to overreact; Mum was right that it didn't count as overreacting if the thing you were fearing was actually quite likely to happen.

Which is why, that Saturday morning, when the element went in the kettle, they both had a point to prove. For Dad he was simply replacing a part; for Mum it had all the makings of a tragedy. The man she loved was about to do battle with electricity and water. It was, quite literally, an elemental struggle. And if she couldn't save him, then at least she could save the rest of us.

With the utmost reluctance, I left Noel Edmonds. David Essex was about to perform his latest single; they couldn't have timed this worse. But I dutifully went to join Mum by the front-garden gate.

'Now what?'

'We wait here until he's done it,' she said. She folded her arms and pursed her lips. 'Why he can't get someone who knows what they're doing to fix it, God knows.'

I pursed my lips too and shook my head in disbelief, since that seemed to be what was called for. But as the minutes ticked by, I started to wonder what exactly Mum thought was going to happen. Did she imagine a big flash-bang explosion the moment he plugged the kettle in? If so, then standing a few yards away at the end of the path probably wouldn't have done much to protect us. Or did she think Dad would be thrown across the room by a powerful shock? Because if that was likely, we ought to be in the house with him to call an ambulance.

I looked at her face, trying to read what else was going on beyond disapproval. If she'd allowed the logical part of her brain to kick in, she would have come to same conclusions I had. So she probably didn't seriously think anything was going to happen. This enforced exodus from the house was a protest, a public vote of no confidence. It was her way of saying, 'If you insist on putting yourself at risk, then I will leave you' – but being Mum, she had no intention of going further than the garden gate and for no more than a matter of minutes.

She turned and saw me scrutinising her.

'What?' she asked, and I could see that her fury with Dad was fading as the ridiculousness of this scenario started to filter through to her.

'Do you think he's OK?'

'He'll be fine,' she said.

'You don't think he's going to blow himself up?'

She gave a half-smile. I don't think it had occurred to her that I might genuinely be scared for him.

'Probably not,' she said, which wasn't the absolute re-assurance I'd hoped for. 'More likely it just won't work. But he needs to learn to stop doing stuff he can't do. He never listens.'

'Can we go back inside then?' I was starting to get a bit cold. And I wondered what the neighbours would be think-ing about us, cowering in our front garden.

'I suppose so,' she said. She gave me a squeeze, then settled the tight-lipped disapproving look back on to her face, ready for when she saw Dad again. At that moment the front door opened and Dad came outside holding two mugs of tea. He handed one to her.

'All right?' he said, with a definite look of triumph.

'I'm not drinking that,' Mum said.

'Why not?'

'You know why,' she said. And walked haughtily back indoors.

Dad handed me the other mug.

'She thought you were going to blow yourself up,' I explained.

'But I didn't, did I? I fixed it. It was only the element. Don't want to get an electrician in for that.'

'I know. But –'

'I did it, Bec. It was perfectly straightforward. Drink the tea. It's nice.'

I took a sip.

'Lovely. Next time, listen to Mum.'

'She worries too much. I know what I'm doing.'

I smiled at him and he started to laugh.

'All right, I don't always. But it worked this time.'

'I think that's the problem. She thinks you'll try to fix everything now.'

"Course I won't,' he said, as if that was a preposterous thing to think.

I gave him a sceptical look.

'Not everything. Maybe ... you know, the odd fuse, a plug, that sort of thing.'

We walked back into the house. Mum had shut herself in the bedroom. Her husband and house were intact, but she needed time to recover from another disaster narrowly averted.

I put the telly on to watch the rest of *Swap Shop*. Dad went into his workroom at the back of the house. After a little while I heard him call my name. He was sitting at his desk, an anglepoise lamp trained on his latest job – a beautiful piece of calligraphy. Around him were bottles of coloured inks, old-fashioned pens with a variety of nibs drying out on pieces of kitchen towel, rulers, pencils, brushes, Stanley knives, rubbers, markers – his toolkit, the one he felt more at home with.

'I'm going to apply gold leaf to this. Want to watch?' he asked. And hunching closer to the paper, holding his breath so that the wisp of pure gold didn't flutter from the handle of his pen, he proceeded to perform an operation of the utmost delicacy. He draped the leaf on to a raised letter, gently dabbed it into position, then began embossing a tiny pattern with the very tip of the nib. When he'd finished he sat up straight and squinted at it.

'Looks all right, doesn't it?'

I put my arm around his shoulders and kissed him on the top of his head.

'I bet none of my friends' dads can do that,' I said.

He grinned up at me and took a sip of his tea.

'All right, Bec,' he said, 'you've made your point.'

Rituals are like phobias. When they're yours, they're of the utmost importance – they fill your head, dominate your time and you can't imagine life without them. But when they're somebody else's they are utterly baffling.

Some time ago, I was in a museum. I often find myself in museums, but that's what happens when you're away filming. You have to fill that downtime somehow, and museums cost less than shopping.

Anyway, I noticed a sign saying 'Japanese Tea Ceremony, this way'. So I followed it, partly because I'm naturally obedient, but mainly because I was curious. I love tea as much as the next Englishwoman, but I can't claim to make it with any ceremony. I sniff the milk to check it's not off, remove the teabag before the top goes scummy, and that's about it. But I'd recently been reading a book about mindfulness – well, hadn't everybody? – and was starting to be aware of the everyday activities that I did without ever really stopping and noticing them. Perhaps I could learn something from this tea ceremony. Maybe, instead of boiling the kettle and glugging a cup down as I answered emails, I could turn tea-making into a positive enhancement of my well-being. And anyway, it was raining, I had the whole day to fill and there was an hour to go before I could reasonably have lunch, so I trotted off to have a look.

The sign directed me to a full-size reconstruction of a traditional Japanese tea room, built like a stage set inside one of the museum's exhibition rooms. The decor was peaceful and minimal with bamboo mats on the floor and screened walls made of wood and paper. There was a small stove and a couple of low tables with bowls and teapots and ladles of differing sizes. And where the fourth wall should have been, there were a few rows of chairs, so I found an empty one at the back and sat down.

After a moment or two, a couple of Japanese women appeared through a door in the back of the set and a third woman, who wasn't Japanese, walked around the outside and positioned herself in front of it. The former wore what I was about to discover were the traditional costumes of the maiko – hikizuri kimonos in jewel-bright silk. The latter wore the equally traditional costume of the British university academic – linen shirt and trousers, sensible shoes and a scarf with a pattern of Van Gogh's Irises from the museum gift shop.

'We'd like to welcome you,' the academic said, 'to this demonstration of the tea ceremony, a fascinating ritual which has been performed since the mid-sixteenth century.'

She introduced the two women in kimonos, who bowed to her but said nothing. Then they took up their opening positions ready for the ceremony to begin.

'Now I wonder if I might ask for a volunteer to be our Shokyaku, or guest of honour?' the academic went on.

Audience participation is a bit of a busman's holiday for me, so I slid down in my chair to avoid making eye contact. But a few rows in front of me an arm shot up with alacrity, and a young man left his chair and was ushered into the set.

Now this reconstruction, we'd been told, was of a Koma – one of the smaller types of tea room. The volunteer, however, was one of the larger types of audience member. He wasn't just large from side to side, but immensely tall with it, and as he stepped into the mocked-up tea room he overfilled it to a cartoonish degree. Think Alice in the White Rabbit's house after she'd drunk the potion, and you'll begin to get the idea.

The two Japanese women must have calculated, as we all had, that their Shokyaku would struggle to kneel on a bamboo mat and that if he did make it down there, he might never get back up again. So one of them ushered him towards a stool instead. But, like everything in the tea room, it was minimal in design. In fact its seat was roughly the size of a paperback novel, so it only made him look the more gigantic as he lowered himself gamely but unsteadily into position.

Once he was settled, the academic began to talk us through the ceremony. It was fascinating and quietly beautiful. Everything, from the presentation of sweets, to the handling of the utensils, to the bowing and kneeling and pouring, was strictly choreographed; nothing was unconsidered, everything was savoured. It was mindfulness exemplified and I promised myself that I would incorporate a little of this from now on the next time I boiled the kettle – unless, of course, I was gasping for a cuppa and *University Challenge* was about to start.

Ten minutes in, though, around the time the Shokyaku appeared to be losing the feeling in his feet, something strange occurred. The academic had stopped to clear her throat a couple of times during her narration, but the croak kept coming back. Now her airways audibly tightened and her voice, having squeaked on for a few more syllables, seized up altogether.

The more she tried to speak, the worse it got, and, after a few more delicate and ultimately fruitless throat-clears, she was seized at last by a choking fit so violent that she simply had to stop. She gestured to the audience to give her a moment and disappeared behind the scenery, removing herself from the peaceful grace of ancient Japan before hawking up the contents of her lungs in the back room of an English museum.

Since this wasn't an actual tea ceremony but an explanation of a tea ceremony, the women in kimonos had performed each section of the ritual only when prompted to by the academic. So when she disappeared, the whole thing stopped. The women stood frozen, eyes lowered, still holding whatever utensils they were about to use. And the poor audience member, clearly afraid that standing up and stretching would be a terrible breach of etiquette, perched in silent agony for what seemed like an eternity. From behind the scenery, the academic could still be heard coughing, throat-clearing, and coughing again. Nobody seemed to know quite what should happen next.

Then, as if a light bulb had lit up in her head, one of the Japanese women suddenly broke character, grabbed a bowl, poured some tea into it and raced round the set to give it to the academic.

The ritual of the ceremony had wrapped us up so thoroughly that, even when someone was evidently in need of a drink, we'd all forgotten there was tea to be had at the end of it.

We Jews have plenty of rituals – I'm not sure there are any for making tea, but there's one for pretty well everything else, if you care to seek them out.

My background, for the avoidance of doubt, is not remotely Orthodox – my dad didn't wear a big black hat and my mum didn't wear a wig. We could read Hebrew a bit, but to roughly the standard of an infant-school child reading English, and we only went to synagogue a few times a year. As a child, I remember my parents being apologetic about the not-going-to-synagogue part. But when I look back on it now, and compare my family with that of other Jews I know, I think we were surprisingly observant. We always kept to a kosher diet, for instance, and we lit candles and said 'kiddush' every Friday night. But we did these things according to our own rules. We didn't light the candles, as tradition dictated, as soon as the sun went down; we did it when dinner was ready, or when we'd done our homework, or when Dad had finished watching the news headlines. We steered a middle course between dedicated adherence and gentle subversion, doing all the same things our ancestors had done, but with a more relaxed attitude.

But those rituals, the lighting of candles and sipping of wine, the saying of some prayers and singing of others, were our markers of passing time, the template we laid over our weeks and months and years. In winter, there was Chanukah, when we lit coloured candles and ate fried foods. In spring it was Purim, with fancy-dress competitions for the kids, and in autumn we'd parade through the synagogue for Sukkot with plaited palm fronds and a giant lemon. I'm not even going to try to explain that one, but trust me, it's a thing. It was absurd in one way, but it also meant something. It held us close to our shared history.

As a child, when I heard people say that religion was the cause of most of the wars in history, I was genuinely baffled. Now, of course, I can see how any kind of tribalism can lead to a hatred of the Other. But it's all a question of degree. It's perfectly possible to love giant lemons and coloured candles, and not to see people who don't as your enemy.

Nonetheless, the non-Jewish world we lived in had its own template, and as I got older I realised that the two didn't quite fit together. It was tricky enough sourcing plaited palm fronds in suburban East London, but trickier still getting time off work to parade them around a synagogue.

When I started my career as an actress, I realised I couldn't stay home with my family every Friday night. Saturday might be the day of rest for Jews, but if you're working in the theatre there's a matinee and an evening show to do. The templates didn't fit, and choices had to be made.

So I took the decision that for 364 days of the year I would do whatever I needed to do for my career, and on the remaining one – Yom Kippur, the holiest of holies, the solemn Day of Atonement – I'd just be a Jew. It hasn't always been straightforward. I have to ask for it to be written into contracts so that it doesn't get swallowed up by ever-changing filming schedules. But my agents have always supported me and so far each year, no matter what I've been doing the day before or where I'm flying off to the day after, on that one day I fast for twenty-five hours, go to synagogue with my family and repent for all the horrible things I've done since the last time I was there.

Sometimes I regret choosing Yom Kippur for this token-istic adherence. It may be the most important festival in the Jewish calendar, but it is also, by a very large margin, the least fun. If I were a fair-weather Jew, I'd have picked Passover instead. A celebration of the biblical exodus from Egypt, Passover takes place in March or April, and though I never take time off work for it, I still try to mark it wherever I am in the world by sticking to its slightly weird diet. The cornerstone of this is matzos: thin, crispy crackers which you'll probably have heard of because they happen to taste nice with cheese. As long as I'm eating matzos and avoiding bread, cake and a handful of other banned foods, I can tell myself I'm *doing* Passover. This abstinence, though, is clearly not the fun part. It's the Seder night, the ceremonial meal with which the week begins, that I really look forward to.

The word 'Seder' means 'order', and it refers to the set pattern the evening has to follow. For my family, it's prob-ably the closest we get to a Japanese tea ceremony in that everything, from food preparation through eating to the celebration after the meal, has to be done in a prescribed way. But the more adherent we try to be, the more we des-cend into confusion and chaos, and that's where the fun begins.

At the centre of the dinner table on a Seder night is a circular plate on which you'll find a curious array of sym-bolic foods. There's an egg with a burnt shell, a bowl of salted water, a clump of parsley, some grated horseradish and a delicious sticky brown mush called haroseth, made from wine and ground nuts and apple. Each of these foods must be tasted at the appropriate point in the service and you don't get to eat your dinner until you've ticked them off your checklist. There's no solemnity to it – it feels more like working your way through a rather odd tasting-menu than performing a religious rite.

In pride of place on the Seder plate is a lamb shankbone, the symbolic representation of the Paschal lamb. Easter and Passover share a lot of the same iconography, and the Hebrew name for Passover – Pesach – is where the word 'Paschal' derives from. So in most Jewish households, this shankbone is regarded as a *sine qua non*. But my family is vegetarian, so to avoid having a chunk of dead animal on our festive table we deploy a shankbone lookalike in the form of a mushroom. Our Seder is therefore hobbled by bathos from the get-go, since it's unlikely that any of the ancient temple rituals involved a sacrificial mushroom.

But that bathos is itself the perfect symbol of Passover, the festival where the mystical and the mundane, the hallowed and the hysterical, sit happily side by side.

You might think that since the particulars of the Seder are written down in a book (the Haggadah) and have been practised in the same way for generations, every evening would be the same. But you'd be wrong.

For one thing, Judaism is a diaspora religion, its adherents have been apart more than they've been together – 2,000 years more, in fact. So the Seder is more like Chinese whispers than a Japanese tea ceremony. Everybody around the table has their own Haggadah and, since these books get passed down from generation to generation, each family may have four or five versions. And here's the knock-out – every Haggadah is slightly and subtly different. So when my Haggadah says I should raise my glass of wine, say a blessing and drink, my mother's might tell her to raise her glass, say the blessing and put the glass down again *without* drinking. My brother's, meanwhile, might say he should leave his glass where it is and not do anything for another page and a half.

In addition to that, because Judaism is a discursive religion in which the truly devout dedicate their lives to minute interpretations of its texts, pages and pages of the Haggadah are spent retelling semantic arguments from history. One rabbi, centuries ago, said the ten plagues were ten plagues, while another rabbi argued that, if you looked at it differently, you could make a case for there actually being twenty plagues, and a third topped it by proving there could have been forty, or fifty, or eighty. These bearded, wise, cussed old boys would have spent their whole lives competing to prove an intellectual point. And at the Seder, even part-time Jews like me are expected to join in.

So giving this thing the name 'Seder' or 'order' is both misleading and, I suspect, intentionally ironic. There is an order to it, but you have to go through chaos to achieve it. It's one part ritual to two parts anarchy.

Perhaps that's why the Japanese tea ceremony had seemed so beguilingly alien to me. All that tranquillity, all that order – I'm just not used to it. The Jewish rituals I grew up with aren't peaceful celebrations of mindfulness.

We don't sit in silence and contemplate the feel of a bowl in our hands or the taste of the tea on our tongues. We spend whole evenings arguing over when to eat a bit of horseradish. The fact that we do these things at a set time every year imposes a kind of order on our lives, but the disordered way in which we do them tells us that the way you practise is less important than the practice itself. To me, as a thoroughly imperfect Jew, who works on Friday nights and can't read Hebrew very well, it makes it all OK somehow.

My Judaism is like Eric Morecambe's version of Grieg's Piano Concerto – I'm playing all the right notes, but not necessarily in the right order.

There's one experience that sums this up perfectly. I was doing a musical in the West End some years ago, and as April approached, I suddenly realised that the Seder night that year (Passover is a movable feast, so the dates change) was a Tuesday. I would be working, and there was no way of getting the night off. I'd known of course that this would happen sooner or later. My parents knew it too and they understood. It was just one of those things. After all, I'd ring-fenced Yom Kippur, as usual. That was my gesture, my nod towards being Jewish. I'd have to miss the Seder and that was that.

But as Passover got closer, I couldn't help feeling a little bit mournful about it. One evening, as I was putting on my make-up before the show, my friend Sophie, with whom I shared a dressing room, asked me if everything was OK.

So I told her about Pesach, and about missing the Seder.

'Is it a bit like Christmas dinner?' she asked.

Kind of, I explained, but kind of . . . not like anything else at all.

We went on stage shortly afterwards and did the show, but Sophie's a naturally curious person, and over the next few days she kept coming back to the conversation – asking me more and more questions about what it entailed and how long it took and what were the essential components.

On the night of the Seder itself, while my family were eating haroseth and bickering about whether to sip or not to sip, I was on stage with Sophie and the rest of the company, singing and dancing our way through Act One. But as the curtain came down for the interval and everyone headed off stage I was waylaid by our stage manager on some flimsy pretext or other. When I finally got to our dressing room, I could hear the occasional giggle and voices being shushed. I opened the door and found the entire cast crammed into the room. On the table was a bottle of wine, some glasses, some candles and a box of matzos.

'Happy Pesach,' Sophie said.

I was touched beyond words, but there wasn't time to get teary. We had an order to get through before the audience came back from the bar.

I lit the candles and said the blessings, everyone tried some matzo and sipped wine. They did so at the same time and without an argument, which seemed a bit weird to me, but it was still somehow comforting. We played all the right notes in whatever order we could manage.

For those few moments backstage, as I tried to explain the component parts of a ritual to people for whom it was as alien as the Japanese tea ceremony was to me, I was more mindful of the meaning of Pesach than I'd probably ever been.

We finished our wine, dusted the matzo crumbs off our costumes, blew out the candles and went back to complete the other ritual of the night – Act Two. And I realised that this was why Sophie and the others had understood the importance of the Seder – because our working lives are all about doing things again and again, following a strict, unchanging order that is always just a heartbeat away from chaos.

That night, under Sophie's guidance, my friends – this family away from family – had shifted the mismatched templates of my life into alignment. It was fifteen minutes in a basement West End dressing room, but a ceremony doesn't have to be perfect to be right.

FRIENDS FOR DINNER

I'm going to say this outright – Phil and I have a lot of dinner parties.

Yes, yes . . . I can sense the eye-rolling already; the weary mumbles of, 'Well, there's a surprise. A middle-class woman who likes dinner parties.' But before you rush to judgement, review that opening sentence. I said we have a lot of dinner parties. I didn't say I enjoyed them. And I didn't say it was my idea.

In fact it's Phil – with his impeccable working-class credentials; Phil, who grew up on a council estate and whose mother used to buy live eels from Brixton market – who instigates them. For him, it's nothing to do with status; it's a simple, uncomplicated pleasure. He loves cooking, and he wants to see people enjoying what he's cooked. He couldn't be less interested in the table dressing, the music, whether the recipes are from some fashionable cookbook. He's perfectly happy with paper towels for napkins and saucepans on the table. He just wants his food to be relished, and he thoroughly enjoys the creative thrill of preparing it.

As a result, our freezer is packed with see-through bags of home-made stock and ragu and soup, and our fridge full of bowls of goose fat and dripping and other globs of gelatinous mystery. I once spotted a jam jar with a small amount of grey, mouldy residue in the bottom and was about to throw it away when I noticed it had a handwritten label that said simply 'MOTHER'. Now it happened that only a few months earlier Phil's mother had died and he and his siblings had yet to settle on a place to scatter her ashes, so for a moment, I stood there, blinking at it in horror, wondering by what perverse logic he had decided that she needed refrigerating. Then Phil came in, asked me what I was doing with his sourdough-bread starter ('mother' apparently is the term the cognoscenti use – see, I'm not middle class *enough*) and put it back in the fridge.

So the dinner party, for Phil, isn't a cliché, it's a joy. Indeed, left to his own devices, he'd gladly turn every night into a sort of open house because he's also much more sociable than I am. I love friends and I love food, so putting the two together should be my ideal too, but frankly, I can take dinner parties or leave them. I rarely complain, because he does most of the work – he plans it, invites the guests, shops, cooks; all I have to do is make sure the toilets aren't an embarrassment, worry about where on the class spectrum it places me if I *call* them toilets, and . . . well, be there. But sometimes, after a long period of filming, for instance, 'being there' is more of a challenge than he has ever fully understood. 'Being there', even with very close friends, involves some level of social engagement. You can't 'be there' while playing online Scrabble. You can't 'be there' and doze off at eight thirty. You can't 'be there' in your dressing gown.

So it was that when, one Monday, after a moderately tiring day at work, Phil suggested that we have a dinner party the next weekend, I mumbled an ambiguous reply, hoping he'd get distracted and the whole notion might go away.

'You always make that noise,' he said, 'because you never want to do it. But then when everyone's gone, you always say we should do it more often.'

'Yes,' I replied, 'that's because everyone's gone. Ask me before they arrive, and you might get a different answer. Then I just feel exhausted, and overwhelmed.'

'But I do everything,' he reminded me. 'How can you be exhausted?'

'It's exhausting watching you. Seeing you zipping around to the shops and back, and chopping and frying and flavouring and perfecting. I look at you unrolling cling film and covering ramekins full of God knows what and frankly I want to lie down.'

Phil narrowed his eyes.

'But you *can*, if you want to. You *can* lie down, because I'm doing everything. Seriously, I'm not asking you to chip in. I *like* doing it all. I'm just asking you to . . . be there.'

And that of course is how I should have left it. OK, he was foisting sociability on me when all I wanted was to slob out, but as selfish acts go, feeding your wife and friends and tidying up afterwards was definitely at the forgivable end of the scale. I should have let it lie; but I wasn't in a letting-things-lie kind of a mood.

'I'm capable of doing it all as well, you know,' I said, and realised immediately that I was starting a row.

'I know,' Phil replied guardedly, because he'd realised it too.

'I mean, I used to have dinner parties before I met you.' I could have added the words 'rarely' and 'reluctantly' but I wasn't in a telling-the-whole-truth kind of a mood, either.

'I know. You're a good cook. Only . . .'

'Only what?' I asked.

'You know . . .'

'What?'

'You used to get a bit . . . erm . . . stressed. If you remember.'

I opened my mouth to rebut this accusation, but a montage of images flitted across my memory: me weeping over a burnt apple flan; storming to the shops in a fury because I'd forgotten to put flour in the chocolate brownies; hitting a TV chef's photo with a wooden spoon after his recipe had defeated me. I closed my mouth again and pursed it this time.

'I'm not blaming you,' he carried on. 'It's not really your thing. But I like doing dinner parties, and I'd like to do one this weekend. Please.'

I didn't say anything straight away. I didn't particularly want this thing to happen, but I also resented the implication – true though it was – that it wouldn't happen if it were up to me. It suddenly occurred to me that the only way I could get the upper hand in this utterly pointless non-argument was to play Phil at his own game. If he could be a relaxed and capable host, then so could I.

'OK. But *I'll* do it,' I said. 'I'll organise the whole thing.'

'Okaaay,' Phil replied, uncertainly.

'You think I've forgotten how to cook, don't you?' I said, still spoiling for a fight.

'No. You cooked the other night. It was lovely.'

'It was broccoli pasta. For the kids. That's not the sort of cooking I'm talking about.'

'Listen,' Phil began, before adding a judicious 'sweetheart', 'I suggested a dinner party because I love doing them. I don't want you to have to make any effort. I'm happy to do it all.'

'It's no effort,' I said, trying to sound breezy through a tight-lipped smile. 'No effort at all. I'll sort it. I'll do the whole thing myself. It'll be fun. I'm looking forward to it actually.' And with that final barefaced lie, it was decided.

The first challenge lay in inviting people. Phil's approach to this is charmingly naïve. He looks through his address book, thinks of people he likes but hasn't seen for a while, texts them with the offer of free food, wine and some entertaining company, and waits for them to say yes. And they usually do, which surprises me. Because I, with what I consider a more sophisticated view of human nature (and what Phil calls paranoia), can't help imagining the conversation that might follow that text:

'Phil and Rebecca have asked us round. Again,' one friend would say.

'I blame you,' the other would reply. 'I said we should find an excuse the first time.'

'I said yes out of pity. I thought it was a one-off. For crying out loud, how thick-skinned can these people be?'

Somewhere in my journey to adulthood, you see, I convinced myself that none of my friends actually wanted to spend time with me. It comes from the feeling that if I were them, I wouldn't want to spend time with me either. That may sound unnecessarily harsh, but try asking yourself the question – if I were someone else, would I want to be friends with me? I mean, it depends what you mean by 'being friends'. The odd phone call, emails, a drink a couple of times a year – yeah, great. I'd be happy with that. But in all honesty, I wouldn't invite me for a whole weekend.

Consequently, now that I had to invite people for dinner, the texts I sent were so full of get-out clauses as to be almost incomprehensible.

Hi, it's me. Rebecca. (Front.) (As in Rebecca and Phil.) Hope you're well. We're having some people round for supper. We know we asked you not long ago and I promise we're not stalking you. But it'd be great if you fancied joining us as you'll probably like the other people who are coming. If these other people don't come, don't worry, we'll keep looking until we find someone else we think you'll like. The main thing is, you won't be stuck with us. Now, the other thing is, I'll be cooking, not Phil. So let me know if you'd rather bring something you've prepared, in case. In fact, no need to let me know, just do it. But there'll be more than enough of what I'm cooking, so you can always change your mind if it looks OK after all. Anyway, totally understand if you can't come. Or would rather not. We'll rearrange for another time. Or not, if you prefer, because like I said we're not stalking you. Lots of love, Rebecca. (Front. Phil's wife.)

Curiously, this approach seemed to have a lower hit rate than Phil's. So after receiving one or two rejections, my suspicion that nobody would want to come had become unarguable fact. I was all ready to call the whole enterprise off when Phil came in from a meeting and said:

'This American producer I was talking to today doesn't really know anyone in London. And she's at a loose end on the night of our dinner party, so I said she could join us. Hope that's OK.'

Great. He'd invited someone I'd never met, a film producer who had the capability of furthering or hindering my career, to be the only guest at a dinner party I was hoping not to have. He'd called my bluff, blocked my escape route. I now had to invite more people. And since all my safe-option invitees – my closest friends and family – were otherwise engaged, I was going to have to take a risk and ask someone I'd never invited before. I looked through the contacts list on my phone again and again, but there always seemed to be a reason not to make the approach. Perhaps they'd said something that had irritated me, or I was worried they'd think I had a crush on them, or I knew they'd start an argument, or I wasn't sure if they were still with their partner. If I invited one single friend they might feel awkward, but two might look like I was matchmaking. And on and on until I'd tied myself up in knots. Eventually I took a deep breath and invited an actor I'd recently worked with. I was pretty sure he was going to be out of the country, but at least I would have shown willing, and maybe if I came up with enough refusals, Phil would uninvite his producer and give up on the whole idea. I could almost picture myself looking regretful, saying 'Well, I gave it my best shot', putting on my slippers and sticking a James Stewart DVD in the machine.

But the actor said yes. And his partner was free too. Even though I'd asked them solely because I thought they wouldn't come, I was actually rather flattered. I told Phil, with a certain air of smugness, that we now had five, including ourselves, coming to *my* dinner party, and three of them had never been round before. I was breaking new ground, taking risks. I was being . . . him.

'Actually, it'll be six, if you don't mind the producer bringing her boyfriend.'

'I thought you said she didn't know anyone in London.'

'She doesn't. He's flying in from Paris.'

'For our dinner party?'

'No. To be with her.'

'And she's bringing him to meet a load of people she doesn't know?' I realised I was sounding shrill again, but somehow I couldn't help it. 'She lives in LA, he lives in Paris. For once they're on the same continent. Shouldn't they be having sex, for God's sake?'

'Maybe they're going to do that after the dinner party,' said Phil patiently. 'Or before. Or potentially both.'

'Well lucky them,' I cried. 'I'll think of them having sex while I'm scrubbing the toilet.'

'Will you?' asked Phil, looking disturbed.

'No. Not literally. I'm just saying it's odd, that's all. Who is this producer again?'

'I told you about her. I had dinner at her father's restaurant when I was in New York.'

I stopped wiping crumbs off the table, which is what I do when I'm getting riled, and stared at him.

'Her father's a restaurateur?'

'Yes.'

'You've invited someone from the catering industry to sample my cooking . . .?'

'*She's* not in catering. Her family are.'

'But she knows about food,' I said in a panicky tone. 'I mean, she'll know if it's no good.'

'She's not a chef, Bec. She's a film producer.'

'Oh well that's OK, then, I suppose.'

Phil turned to leave the room, pausing only to mumble, nervously:

'It's her boyfriend who's a chef.'

The actor hated fish. He told me this in reply to my 'Anything you can't eat?' text, and since I don't eat meat, that was two major protein sources ruled out straight off the bat. But it got worse. His partner didn't eat spinach, mildly disliked beetroot and, although he wasn't strictly speaking allergic, he'd once had a nasty turn after eating some sweet peppers. The chef would eat anything, apparently, though I was pretty sure I could knock that out of him. And the producer was also easy to please, only she hated coriander. Hated it. I checked her message several times, to make sure. It seemed such an odd thing to hate. Coriander: possibly the least offensive of all foodstuffs. I could understand not wanting to eat a whole bunch of it; not wanting an entire meal of nothing but coriander, but hating it, outright, every single measly leaf of the stuff . . . that smacked of attention-seeking to me.

I flicked disconsolately through the cookery books I had left once I'd rooted out the meaty ones, the fishy ones and the niche ones for coriander lovers. Pies – too hearty. Quiches – too retro. Anything 'on a bed of' something else – too much faff. I tried to think of a signature dish, something I'd cooked frequently that had never let me down, but since most of my recent cooking had been for the kids, the closest I had to a signature dish was fish fingers with ketchup and rice. I turned another page.

'Gnocchi', I read, 'is an unusual alternative to pasta and is surprisingly easy to make from scratch.'

Home-made gnocchi. That had just the right sound to it. 'It's home-made gnocchi,' I could hear myself saying as I brought it to the table in a peasant-style, earthenware serving dish. 'I made it myself. At home. Oh really, you've never made gnocchi from scratch?' And here I'd allow myself a self-deprecating smile. 'It's surprisingly easy.'

I liked this idea, so I read through the recipe and it did indeed look straightforward. I could serve it with a nice sauce and a vegetable side dish which carefully avoided beetroot, spinach, sweet peppers and bloody coriander. I bought all the ingredients, did as much preparation as it was possible to do the day before, and went off to clean the toilets, while avoiding thinking about a couple I'd never met before having sex.

At 7.30 p.m. on Saturday, the kids were fed and happy, the house cleaned and the kitchen table cleared of newspapers, bits of old lunch and the Mayan temple made from a Coco Pops box which had sat there for nearly a month. The best crockery was out and five of the six wine glasses, though dishwasher milky, were roughly the same size. It had all been a breeze.

I decided, for the avoidance of last-minute panic, to do a quick test run with the gnocchi, which were sitting in their raw state, lightly dusted with flour and looking, frankly, beautiful. I casually dropped a couple into a small pan of boiling water and waited for them to bob to the surface. But no bobbing occurred. I left it a few moments longer than the recipe suggested, thinking perhaps that, being out of practice, I had mistaken a rolling boil for a fast boil or even, heaven forbid, a simmer. Still no sign of the gnocchi. I took a slotted spoon and rootled around in the bottom of the pan. The pert nuggets of dough I'd lovingly crafted seemed to have disappeared. In their place was a mass of stringy, grey gloop. I fished it out and put it on a plate. It looked like chewing gum, or a distressingly chalky cowpat. I stared at it, half hoping that it might miraculously separate out into two nice, neat, golden gnocchi again. It didn't of course, and as it cooled it began to look like the sort of elastic you'd find in a pair of elderly pants.

'You've never made gnocchi from scratch?' said the taunting voice of nemesis. 'It's surprisingly easy.'

Phil walked in, looking crisp and fresh and smelling of cologne. He'd had a lovely day, relaxing with the children while I, as promised, had done everything for once. On his way up to get changed, he'd cast an approving eye over the preparations and remarked that it was a bit like old times.

'Only without the last-minute panic,' I'd said, jauntily, and we'd both enjoyed the memory of how stressed the younger me used to get.

'Shall we crack open a bottle?' he said now and gave me an affectionate peck on the cheek. I remained motionless, staring at the blob.

'What's that?' he asked.

'Dinner,' I said grimly.

He put the bottle of wine down and poured me a large vodka.

'Right,' he said in a reassuring tone. 'It's not a disaster. We've got a starter . . . and . . . some bread.'

I knocked back the vodka and glowered at him, like it was all his fault.

'Do you want *me* to –'

'No,' I barked before he'd had a chance to finish.

'We could order a –'

'No,' I said again, only louder this time.

'Well, Bec, it's just . . . they're going to be here any minute so . . .'

'I KNOW that,' I said.

'. . . So we need to make a decision. I mean they've come to see *us*, don't forget. The food is the least important part of it.' He was wittering now, his voice getting slightly hysterical as he rummaged through cupboards looking for something we could knock up in a hurry.

I, on the other hand, had suddenly been suffused with an eerie calm. The vodka had kicked in, and with it the realisation that it wasn't the end of the world, that there were people starving and homeless and trapped in war zones who'd be only too delighted if the worst they had to deal with was the lack of a suitable main course. I went to the cupboard and drew out six ramekins.

'What are you going to do with those?' Phil asked, as though I was holding live grenades.

'I'm going to make soufflés,' I replied.

'Oh shit,' Phil murmured, and at that moment the doorbell rang.

Some years prior to this evening, Phil had been sent to a management training seminar where he had learned about the Critical Path Method. This is a technique for making projects more manageable by dividing them, as far as I understand it, into their component parts or activities, figuring out in what order you need to do those activities and how long each one will take, and then getting yourself organised accordingly. We had, as a couple, learned three things following the arrival of the Critical Path Method in our lives:

1. Phil could apply it to anything, being essentially logical, methodical and patient.
2. I could apply it to nothing, being conversely illogical, scattergun and easily irritated.

And:

3. That it was a good term to have in your lexicon when you wanted to accuse the other of being any of the above.

The point is that soufflés are not, contrary to their reputation, the hardest things in the world to make, but they do depend entirely on the application of the Critical Path Method. There's no point whisking your egg whites before you've made your roux, or putting the oven on after you've transferred the mixture to the dishes. It's all perfectly workable, but you need a clear head, a strong nerve and the ability to multi-task. At the very best of times, I possess none of those qualities. Now, drunk on vodka and champagne, trying to make something edible out of nothing much for a French chef, the scion of a Los Angeles catering dynasty and a guy who's so unadventurous he won't even risk a pimento, it was madness even to try.

The guests, unaware of the lack of a main course, were having a fine old time. They had bonded nicely and were laughing and chatting and drinking, for all the world as if this were a dinner party, rather than what it was more likely to be – an evening of sitting around a table getting peckish. Only Phil was uneasy; he had the ramrod back and tight jaw of a man for whom life in the next few hours wasn't going to be much fun. I stood by the cooker whisking and grating and stirring like I knew what I was doing, occasionally stealing a look at a recipe, mopping sweat from my brow and mumbling expletives under my breath. But at every stage, it looked the way it was meant to look. The sauce thickened and the egg whites stiffened and the ingredients seemed mysteriously to believe that I was in control.

When the mixture had been doled out into the ramekins, I took a deep breath and bunged them in the oven. There was nothing more I could do now. If they didn't work, there was no alternative. The fridge was empty, and the kids had finished off the fish fingers.

I needed a moment to compose myself, so I went to the bathroom and splashed my face with cold water. I looked in the mirror. My hair had frizzed up from the heat of the kitchen, and my mascara had smudged. I tidied myself up and headed back downstairs. It must be nearly time for the soufflés to come out, I thought, but in my tipsiness I couldn't quite remember how long I'd set the timer for. In fact, I suddenly realised, I couldn't remember setting the timer at all.

I hurtled down the last few stairs. I could smell burning, but it could have been the remnants of the fish fingers crisping up on the oven shelf. I threw open the kitchen door.

'Ah there you are,' said the chef. Both he and Phil were on their feet. 'Phil said you hadn't set the timer, but I told him that a real soufflé expert judges it by smell.'

I shot Phil a look of desperation. It matched the one he was already wearing. Then I opened the oven door and pulled out the tray.

Six dreamy, golden, puffy soufflés wobbled slightly as I brought them to the table. The guests sighed appreciatively. Phil let slip an involuntary 'Oh, thank God.'

Everybody started eating.

'Perfect,' said the chef.

'Delicious,' said the producer.

'*We* should have more dinner parties,' the actor's partner said. 'But it's all too high stress for me.'

'Yes,' said the actor. 'We end up having rows.'

Phil and I smiled as if rowing was an alien concept to us.

'And I'd never even attempt a soufflé,' the actor said. 'Way too fiddly.'

'They're actually . . . surprisingly easy,' I said. And catching sight of the empty vodka glass next to the cooker I added, 'If you're relaxed enough.'

'It's about planning too,' said the chef. 'What's the phrase you use, darling?' he said to the film producer.

'Critical Path Analysis,' she replied. 'It was Phil who told me about it actually.'

Phil shot me a sheepish grin. But I was lost in my own

thoughts, planning the critical path of my next dinner party. It began:

1. Stop being paranoid and invite people.
2. Let Phil do everything, if he wants to.
3. Be there.

GIRLS' NIGHT OUT

Maybe I was over-thinking this. I mean, who makes up these rules? Who says a woman over forty can't wear a short dress? If it looks good, it looks good. And this looked . . . well, definitely not bad. And potentially . . . from the right angle . . . in a dim light . . . with the right shoes . . . potentially almost good. Or maybe it *was* too short. It was difficult to tell this close to the mirror. I could open the curtain and step further away, but that would mean going out into the shop, being seen in public in a dress in which I wasn't yet ready to be seen in public. I leant my head back instead, but that didn't work of course. You can't get an objective view of how something looks on you by arching backwards. So I stood upright again and as far from the mirror as I could get. Too short. Definitely. And yet, with the right shoes . . .

My phone bleeped inside my bag. I bent down to rummage for it, glancing at myself as I did so. Even in this position the dress hung well. It didn't bunch or ruck up. And the colour was unusual. Plus I could afford it, at a push, and I'd been working hard. I should get it – treat myself. I could wear it to the next girls' night out. Yes, if the girls were here, they'd definitely tell me to go for it.

I found the phone and checked to see what had come in. A text. Karen's number. But the message, confusingly, was from her husband, Bill. 'Please forgive me texting you all, but I thought I ought to tell you . . .'

I read it through three or four times. I couldn't reply; not yet. I wanted to talk to someone – Phil maybe or one of the others who would have got the same message. But I couldn't do that yet either. First, I had to take off this absurd dress, pull on my own clothes and get the hell out of the changing room. It wasn't a day for shopping. It wasn't a day for looking in mirrors and wondering if I'd put on a few pounds. It was a bad day, a horrible day, the shittiest of shitty days.

We hadn't gone looking for friendship, just gravitated towards each other: a mixed group of unconnected women brought together by coincidences of location and fertility. We all lived in the same part of town, and our children were in the same class at school. That was it. There were, of course, plenty of other parents who ticked the same two boxes, but they were never to be more than nodding acquaintances, while we became a gang. Initially it was Laura and me. We caught each other's eye on the first day our boys entered Reception class and exchanged a few pleasantries about the weather and where we lived. I thought she seemed nice – a bit reticent, but then so was I. It was all new and unfamiliar. I didn't know the protocol – should you make an effort to be friendly, or was it OK to stand on your own, checking emails on your phone and keeping yourself to yourself? I suspected you were meant to mingle for the sake of your kids. There were playdates to be organised, weren't there? I didn't want to rely on my children making friends all by themselves; they might turn out to be as antisocial as their mother. And there were more practical, self-serving considerations, like finding people you could trust to hold on to your kids if you were running late to pick them up. I'm not a natural at networking, but if it would help keep my children safe, I was prepared to give it a go. So Laura and I had our slightly awkward chats in the playground every day – small talk, hairdresser conversation, no more than passing the time.

After a while though, we found each other's sense of humour, and the chats became more relaxed, more intimate, more gossipy. And gradually other parents would amble over and join in. There was Anna, who'd been living abroad and wanted to find new friends for her son now that she'd taken him away from his old ones. Then there was Anna's neighbour Jess, who had a daughter, and the daughter's best friend's mum, whose name was Karen.

I loved Karen straight off the bat. It was impossible not to. She saw the funny in everything. You'd tell her something quite mundane and she'd hoot with laughter and add to your story with a host of extra punchlines. She made me feel like I was the wittiest person she'd ever met, and there is no surer way to my heart than that. But she was also kind and thoughtful. She worked in property, and when my parents decided to put their house on the market, she bombarded me with information, dos and don'ts, links to websites and recommendations of reputable estate agents. She wanted to make everything all right for everybody, so that we could all stop worrying and have more fun.

And that's what we did, in a simple, uncomplicated way. We were friends because our children were friends. And before we knew it, we were friends because we were friends. We were the 'mums', a gang – a clique, I suppose, but the good kind. When one of us had a birthday or a new job or a free evening, we'd hook up. We went to the pub or had a curry or somebody cooked a main course and somebody else brought pudding. After Phil and I had our kitchen done, the 'mums' were my first proper guests. They had to climb over piles of builders' tools to get to the table, but they all said how marvellous it looked, and pretended not to notice the thin film of dust on their plates. After dinner, Karen excused herself because there was a football match on TV. She joined my son, Ollie, on the sofa and shouted her head off at the ref. She was his mate that night, as much as mine.

Years passed like this, with us sharing our milestones. If it was December, it was Jess's birthday. In July it was Laura's. The kids got bigger and drifted in and out of each other's favour, but the mums just kept on keeping on.

And it was at one of these gatherings – Anna's birthday, I think, in the Thai place up the road – that Karen told us her news.

The first headline that night was that Jess was pregnant again. We were thrilled at the prospect of having another baby around, now that our own kids were coming to the end of primary school. Karen was the most excited of all of us – her youngest was only six months old, so Jess's new baby would have a ready-made playmate. And anyway, she said, she needed something to celebrate because she'd been diagnosed with cancer.

'It's not the worst news,' she explained. 'Well, it's not exactly the best, let's be honest, but there are lots of options and everybody's optimistic.'

I can't remember what we said. Variations on a theme of perkiness, I suppose. That's what people always offer, isn't it? It'll be fine. My cousin had it and she's off climbing Kilimanjaro. It's amazing what they can do these days. She probably wasn't listening to any of it, and neither were we. We were all thinking of the three little kids who depended on her, the husband who adored her. We were thinking what it would be like to be her right now, having to wake up every day and remember it wasn't a nightmare; that there was actually something there inside her, needing to be ex-cised. And while we were thinking of all these things, we were thinking of ourselves, and of the knot of friendship we'd created.

It was true about the cousin getting better, and the amaz-ing things they could do these days. But it wasn't true for Karen. One treatment led to another and another. She lost her hair, the steroids puffed her up and made it hard for her to walk. She came to my birthday get-together at the pub on the high road. It was up a hill, it turned out, though one so shallow that none of us had ever even noticed it before. We only realised now because Karen could hardly make it to the top, but we all pretended it was steeper than it was, and that every one of us was struggling.

She never complained – at least not to us. Occasionally we'd drag it out of her, make her say what a complete pain in the arse it all was, so that she knew she could moan if she wanted to. But she didn't, and we respected that.

And when she mentioned the pain in her collarbone that

might have just been a stiff neck, we all reassured her that she must have slept awkwardly or sat in a draught. But she knew it had spread to her bones and so did we. I don't remember it being said. It didn't have to be. The worst was happening and still we were trying to sound perky because we were her friends and what the hell else could we do?

I hadn't bought that dress that day, which was a shame really. When it came to the funeral, the mums decided to wear bright colours and it would have been perfect. We sat together in the church, our gang – what was left of it. Some of the husbands were there too, but we barely noticed them. Even within our little group, each of us was actually alone. Karen's husband, Bill, tried to marshal their three kids into a pew, but the younger two wanted to run up and down the aisle waving at all the people they knew. Nobody was going to tell them off. They didn't have a mother any more, they might as well have some fun. An older lady, Karen's mother, I assumed, tottered behind them in unfamiliar shoes and a jacket she'd bought for special occasions. She probably imagined wearing it for a theatre trip or Christmas drinks. Not this. Never in your worst nightmare would you think of this. It was she, I guessed, who'd combed the boys' hair and put on their suits and ties. Karen's daughter – the eldest child, who was ten and the same age as Ollie – looked small and pale and numb. We'd each tried to talk to her on the way in, but none of us knew what to say.

It was an upbeat service. No mournful hymns. None of the wallowing in grief that I was used to in Jewish funerals. This was bright, shiny, smiley Anglican grief. The person you loved was on their way to the glory of heaven. Why the long faces? Perhaps it made it easier for people to keep it together, but I needed the catharsis of at least one gloomy tune. Some minor-key organ music and earth-and-worms morbidity would have helped lance the boil of our misery.

When it finished, the vicar invited everyone along to the nearest pub, where Bill had arranged a buffet lunch for us all. There were polite smiles as he said it: a priest asking you to go to the pub in the middle of the day, whatever next? A bit of light relief, a further deflection, look on the bright side, life goes on, mustn't grumble.

As we shuffled out of the east door and into the Victorian graveyard, the mums huddled together. The husbands peeled off to give us some space and everyone else headed straight for the pub. Soon it was just us, the remnants of the gang, ambling along in silence.

Anna spoke first.

'Well, it was a lovely service,' she said. And everyone agreed it had been.

'I don't think the kids have taken it in yet,' said Jess.

'I'm not sure any of us has,' Laura murmured.

I couldn't speak. I knew if I did I'd start to cry and they were all being so stoical and brave that it would have felt ostentatious. In all honesty, I hadn't seen very much of Karen in her final few months. I'd been working hard, doing ridiculous hours. But that wasn't a good enough excuse. I hadn't been there for her because I didn't know what to do or say. I hadn't earned the right to be the first to cry. At least that's what it felt like to me.

But when I looked at Laura, I could see her eyes were full, so I slowed and put my arm around her, and as we hugged the others came and joined us.

Perhaps it was because I was angry at myself that I suddenly found I was shouting – well maybe not shouting exactly. It was hallowed ground after all. I didn't want to wake up the 'Mauds' and 'Alberts' and 'Marys late of this parish', but I was angry. Not just sad but furiously, uncontrollably angry.

'I mean what the fuck is that all about?' I heard myself say. 'Those little kids . . . and . . . Bill . . . and her mum. She was lovely, Karen. She was a good person. She never did a bad thing in her life. Not that I know of. So what's the fucking point in her dying? I mean what does it achieve, how does it help the world? It's stupid. Wasteful and stupid and . . . ' I'd calmed myself down now and was running out of angry words, so I just said 'stupid' again, and it felt like a let-down.

Jess nodded and said quietly, 'It is. You're right. It's completely fucking stupid.'

We'd never heard her swear before, and there was something about her doing it in a churchyard of all places that suddenly seemed absurd.

We started to laugh – proper, guttural, inappropriate laughs. The sort of laughs that Karen used to love. And then we linked arms and walked to the pub. We stayed there until the sun went down, on a table together, isolated from everyone else.

Our group. Our gang. Another milestone. Another girls' night out.

SPEAKING PEACE SLOWLY

I was sitting alone in the back seat of a strange man's car, waiting to see what would happen next. For the previous half an hour we'd hurtled together, this man and I, through the featureless backstreets of a Czech suburb. I had no seat belt and was clutching my flight bag on my lap because every time I put it on the seat he'd take a corner on two wheels and it would fall to the floor. As soon as I'd got in, I'd begun to wonder if he was actually my driver at all. I'd never visited Eastern Europe before, and I'd watched an awful lot of John le Carré thrillers, so I was on a heightened state of alert. OK, this man had been standing in Arrivals with a handwritten sign saying 'BBC', but how did I know he wasn't a spy? I started leafing nervously through the phrase book, hoping to find out how to say 'Please don't hurt me', or at least 'I would prefer not to go so fast'. But then I remembered that reading in the back seat always makes me car-sick, so I tried instead to figure out how I could force open the back door and escape at the next traffic light. I'd just removed a hairpin ready to pick the lock when he swerved to a halt outside a low-rise apartment building.

'You wait,' he said. And he got out and went inside.

I wound down my window. From somewhere nearby I could hear martial music playing on a radio. Should I run? And if so, where to? I also had to allow for the possibility that I was catastrophising. I do that a lot, and how embarrassing would it be if I ran away from the man who had genuinely been sent to pick me up?

As the martial music was reaching its brassy crescendo, my driver appeared again.

'You come,' he said briskly.

I got out of the car and followed him. It didn't feel like a good idea – if this was a TV drama, I'd have been shouting at the screen by now – but I wasn't sure what else to do.

He took me through a passageway and round to the back entrance of the apartment building, buzzed an entryphone and said something in Czech. The door opened and we went inside. The stairwell smelled of bleach, and I wondered if someone had been cleaning up blood spatter.

We went through a door on the first floor, and a smiling young woman in a housecoat shook me warmly by the hand.

'Hello, hello. Welcome. Hello. You please come here.'

She ushered me into a living room, small and neat, and slightly overfilled with heavy furniture.

'Please, please,' she said, pointing to sofa.

'I am Rebecca,' I said as I sat down. I thought it might clarify, if this did turn out to be a Mafia hit, that I was not the intended target.

'Yes,' she said, and beamed at me. 'Me, Maria.'

'Hello, Maria,' I said. We smiled at each other dumbly for a moment. Then she said, 'Eat?'

'Oh, no, I'm fine, thank you,' I replied.

'Yes, eat,' she said again.

'I ate on the plane,' I explained, and did a little mime for both 'eating' and 'plane'. My drama-school training hadn't been a waste after all.

She disappeared into the hallway and exchanged a few hurried words with the driver. The front door slammed and, assuming he must have left, I breathed a sigh of relief. Maria didn't seem like the murdering kind. And anyway she was smaller than me and I reckoned I could take her if things got tough. Just to be on the safe side though, I moved to the armchair facing the door, so that I'd see if she lunged at me with a breadknife. A few moments later she came back into the room carrying a tray with some tea, a saucer of sliced lemons and a plate groaning with meat.

'You friends,' said Maria, frowning and trying to find the words, 'not home. But later . . .'

I guessed she was trying to tell me that the rest of the group were out and that this was where I was to wait for them.

She proudly pointed to the meat plate.

'For my friends?' I asked.

'For you,' she beamed.

'Oh, I couldn't . . .' I began to say. But I saw her face fall.

'Yes. All. You wait long. You eat,' she said again.

I'd forgotten about the spy thriller now; I was no longer catastrophising. I was just trying to figure out how, in very simple English, to break the news to this generous young woman that I was a vegetarian.

Once you'd gone through Bush House's grand portico and navigated your way past security, it started to look like any other office building. You passed the lifts, turned left, out into a courtyard-turned-car park, and back in through a side entrance to an unassuming corridor. The ladies' loos, another set of lifts, a storeroom for cleaning supplies and there you were.

Bush House was, back then, the home of the BBC's World Service – a benevolent throwback to Britain's imperial past. It broadcast programmes twenty-four hours a day, 365 days of the year, to pretty well every country on the planet. At that time, around 170 million people either tuned in or had the option of tuning in. You could listen to its news, current affairs and drama on a shortwave radio in the jungle, or as you bumped along a desert road in a truck. Some people listened clandestinely, their transistors stuffed under a pillow so the neighbours wouldn't hear and report them. Others listened nostalgically – the expats mainly, tuning in for the cricket scores or the news or to hear an English voice that would remind them of home. The BBC was (and still is, by and large) trusted. It had a reputation for authority, reliability and impartiality. Its motto is 'Nation Shall Speak Peace Unto Nation', and the World Service made that possible.

Some decades before my first arrival there, someone had come to the conclusion that there wasn't much point speaking peace unto nations if they didn't understand what you were saying. And so it was decided that a small percentage of this overseas output should be allocated to the teaching of English. The department now making these programmes was colloquially known (insofar as it was known about at all) as E by R – English by Radio.

E by R was like an autonomous sub-state – the Vatican City to the World Service's Rome. There were producers, editors, writers and broadcast assistants whose only job was to come up with the best English-teaching programmes possible. And to deliver those programmes, they employed a group of actors – the E by R Rep.

Surprisingly, considering all the peace-speaking they had to do unto all those nations, there were only six actors at any one time: three men – one young, one middle-aged and one older, and three women – ditto.

I was barely a year out of drama school. So far, I'd done a lot of performances on the cabaret circuit and a brief tour of Italian and Spanish secondary schools with a theatre group that, like E by R, also specialised in English-language teaching. I had my Equity card (without which you couldn't work back then) and an agent. But I hadn't done anything you might call proper acting. Indeed, a casual observer, with no more evidence to go on than how I spent my days, might have mistaken me for someone who made up mail-order parcels in the basement of a posh perfume shop.

I was going out with Aidan, one of the actors I'd met on the tour, and I hope he won't take it amiss when I say that it was when he decided to dump me that my life took an upward turn. I'm sure he won't, in fact, since I know for a fact that his did too.

We were woefully mismatched. For a start, he lived on the thirteenth floor of a tower block and I'm a lift-avoidant claustrophobic. So even popping in for a coffee meant either a massive hike or a full-on panic attack. But it was more than that. Aidan was charming and funny, but apart from sharing a profession, we had absolutely nothing in common. We could argue about anything – what film to go and see, what to have for dinner, whether Buddy Holly's songs were as good as The Beatles' – and each argument followed the same pattern. One of us would make an apparently uncontentious statement, the other would assume they were joking because no one but an idiot could possibly think that, and that would be it for the rest of the evening. Then one day Aidan remembered how much happier he'd been with his previous girlfriend, which even *I* could have told him if he'd ever thought to ask, and he decided to go back to her.

He came to the perfume shop, took me out to lunch and told me it was over, and I imagine that it was as he watched me descending with shredded dignity into my cellar full of cardboard boxes and bubble wrap, that he took pity on me and offered me a lifeline. Because as it happened, Aidan was in full employment as Male Actor (Young) on the E by R Rep, and that very week Female Actor (Young) had announced she was leaving to do *Rookery Nook* in Frinton. There was a vacancy for someone with exactly my skill set and experience, and Aidan very decently suggested that I should try out for it.

I made a voice demo tape and sent it in. There were twelve E by R producers, and the rule was that all of them could vote on whether this was the voice they were looking for. Eleven of them approved me, the one who didn't being a guy called Phil who some years later I would marry. It may seem an odd sort of revenge, but trust me, it's been effective.

Apparently he'd fallen for my attempt to lose all traces of my Essex accent, and was concerned that I sounded too posh.

Anyway, no thanks to Phil, I began my renewable three-month contract as Female Actor (Young), and I couldn't have been more excited. I was working at the BBC – not, admittedly, in a bit that anybody in Britain had heard of, but still closer to living the dream than when I was gift-wrapping bottles of eau de toilette.

To me, every day at E by R was exciting, involving as it did talking into an actual microphone in an actual studio at the actual BBC. On my first day, I got to record some 'drama inserts'. These were short scenes in simple English which would be inserted into a programme to illustrate a teaching point. If, for example, the programme was teaching listeners how to express preferences, one of the rep actors would be a shopkeeper, another a customer, and the scene might run something like this:

Customer: Good morning.
Shopkeeper: Hello. Can I help you?
Customer: Yes. I'd like to buy a newspaper and a chocolate bar, please.
Shopkeeper: Certainly. Would you like milk chocolate or dark chocolate?
Customer: I'd prefer milk chocolate, please.
Shopkeeper: Which newspaper would you like to buy? *The Times* or the *Guardian*?
Customer: I'd prefer the *Telegraph*, please.
Shopkeeper: There you are. That will be £1.45, please.
Customer: May I pay you with a cheque?

Shopkeeper: I'd prefer cash, please.
Customer: There you are then. Thank you.
Shopkeeper: Thank you. Goodbye.

OK, it wasn't an excoriating Royal Court drama – though we'd sometimes inject a bit of Pinteresque subtext for fun – but for a woman still blinking in the sunlight from the mail-order cellar, it was definite progress. And more than anything, it was educational – not just for the listeners, but for me too. My co-stars on that first day were Stephen and Tony, Male Actors Middle-Aged and Older respectively. These guys had been working in radio studios their whole lives and were incredibly generous in training up the newcomer. They taught me how to execute a silent page turn (a skill I still pride myself on today), how to do an approach on mic (from no more than a few steps away, so you don't sound like you've materialised suddenly from another room) and how to turn your head slightly to the left or right of the mic to avoid making a popping sound on the letters 'b' and 'p'. By the end of that first session, I'd learned things that would stand me in good stead throughout my career, and I thank them from the bottom of my heart.

In addition to these inserts, I got to lend my voice to various 'slow-speed' programmes. In these, a presenter would explain the language of a news item, say, or the lyrics of a pop song. And one of the actors on the Rep would read out the phrases slowly and clearly as they were discussed.

Presenter: So, in the song, Phil Collins describes his love as . . .
Me: Groovy.

Presenter: He says . . .

Me: (slowly) Baby, you and me / Got a groovy kind of love.

Presenter: Or more correctly . . .

Me: (slowly) Baby, you and *I* / *Have* a groovy kind of love.

Presenter: Now let's look at the word 'groovy' and how you can use it.

I was taught how to time a Repeat Pause. If you're learning a language online or on a CD, you can press 'pause' whenever you need to. But on the radio, with no such facility, you still need time to practise what you've learned. So there was a strict technique to adhere to. I had to say the word or phrase out loud, then *silently* repeat it in my head but with the word 'beat' before and after it, before saying it out loud again.

Presenter: Now let's look at the word 'groovy' and how you can use it.

Me: Groovy. (*Beat. Groovy. Beat.*) Groovy.

And finally there was the ultimate challenge – the bilingual programmes. In these shows, a presenter from one of the World Service's many foreign-language sections would present the show in their native tongue. My job, given that I was unlikely to understand what they were saying, was to sit there and wait to be nodded at, then to read the next line of the script in English. If you got it right, it would sound like a conversation in two separate languages. The foreign presenters always spoke flawless

English – in fact many of them spoke it far more correctly than any of us did. I loved the ease with which they would switch between the two languages, from rattling through a paragraph in Thai, say, to asking the producer an arcane question about grammatical structures in English. Some of them liked to get the English 'voice' to top and tail the show in their own language too. So I learned to say 'hello' and 'thank you and goodbye' in Sinhalese, Swahili, Thai, Hungarian, Brazilian Portuguese and countless others. I'd listen to the presenter and try to say my meagre few words in as perfect a copy of their accent as possible. It was all brilliant fun.

My time spent at E by R was among the happiest of my career, not just because I was in regular work, and certainly not because it was artistically fulfilling. But there was something intoxicating about showing my BBC pass every morning and being allowed into Bush House; about learning on the job and being surrounded by funny, sparky, talented people all day, every day. I made friends who have stayed with me through the decades.

And, as I mentioned earlier, I met Phil. Our early courtship was conducted in those offices, leaving notes in each other's pigeonholes, hoping our paths would cross in the studio. Nobody else knew at the beginning, at least not until I confided in Female Actor (Middle-Aged), after which word got round pretty fast.

Being part of the World Service broadened my suburban horizons. When Phil and I sat in Bush House's basement bar watching the First Gulf War unfold on TV screens, we were surrounded by producers and presenters whose families were on the front line. Not only was I part of an acting community, I was part of an international community too.

My three-month contract was renewed and renewed again, and as I was approaching my last few weeks on the rep two things happened. Firstly we were told that for the first time ever E by R was going on tour, taking its programmes on the road to schools and regional theatres in what was then Czechoslovakia. And secondly I landed my first TV job.

The rest of the rep and two producers flew out on Monday, while I was still filming my new series. I flew out alone the following day, and was met at Prague airport by a driver with a sign that said 'BBC' on it.

My hostess had returned to the kitchen, leaving me with the plate of meat. I sat and looked at it, wondering if I should stuff it in my luggage, throw it out of the window or eat it for the sake of politeness and to hell with a lifetime of abstinence.

Before coming out here we'd been briefed by someone from the Czech-language service at the BBC. She'd explained that as her country was emerging from its Soviet past, it wasn't a land of hardships, just not one of infinite choices. Food was plentiful but limited in variety. When I asked her how I'd fare as a vegetarian, she'd laughed and said, 'Take emergency rations.'

So I knew that for this young woman to offer me such an array of meat would have taken effort and money, and I desperately wanted to avoid offending her.

I suddenly came up with an idea.

'Maria?' I called, and she came into the room.

'On the plane,' I began and I did my little mime again

as it seemed to have worked last time. 'I ate some food . . .' (more miming).

'Yes,' said Maria. 'But . . .' and she pointed again at the meat.

'But the food on the plane made me sick,' I lied. And for good measure I mimed, food, plane and sick. The penny dropped.

'Oh!' Maria exclaimed. 'You sick?'

I didn't want her to think I was going to throw up on the furniture, I just needed her to put the precious meat back in the fridge so it wouldn't go to waste.

'Now, I feel good,' I said, giving a thumbs-up. 'But I will not eat. Thank you.'

She smiled at me sympathetically, picked up the plate of meat and carried it out of the room.

I felt relieved. I hadn't been murdered and I'd avoided a diplomatic incident. Now perhaps I should get on with what I was actually sent here to do – teaching English.

Maria came back into the room.

'Tea OK?' she asked, and pointed at my stomach.

'The tea is lovely,' I said.

'Water?' said Maria, and I seized my opportunity.

'I like water,' I said with the thumbs-up gesture again, 'but I *prefer* tea.'

I waited a beat, allowing her to repeat it in her head, then after one more beat I said, 'I like water, but I *prefer* tea.'

Maria nodded, processed what I'd said, and with a precision my E by R producers would be proud of she said:

'You prefer tea?'

'Yes,' I said.

'Good,' she said, and looked rightly pleased with herself.

'You speak good English, Maria,' I said.

'Good?' She grinned.

'Really good.' I gave her another encouraging thumbs-up and then, because I couldn't resist, I added:

'Groovy.'

DOES THIS FEEL WEIRD TO YOU?

The nurse thought music would relax me. Well, she'd never met me before. In the state I was in, the only thing that would help was the sedative I'd been promised, and the quicker they gave it to me the better. But it was a kind offer and I didn't want to be churlish, so I said yes please to the music.

'What do you like?' she asked.

'Jazz, maybe?' I said.

'Trad, avant-garde or be-bop?' she asked.

I couldn't help being impressed. Admittedly, if I'd gone private there'd have been a quartet in the room with me, dressed in scrubs and muting their trumpets with those cardboard vomit bowls, but you've got to hand it to the NHS, they do their best with limited resources.

'Nothing too . . . jangly,' I said.

'Jangly?'

'You know . . . spiky, atonal. Nothing that's going to make me even more tense.'

The nurse looked thoughtful and started jabbing numbers on a keypad, looking perhaps for a radio station called

Jazz for the Anxious. It occurred to me we could by now have been halfway through the procedure, so to hurry things along I said:

'Or better still, classical. Something soothing. Classic FM.'

'Got you,' said the nurse.

Music started to fill the room.

It would be an overstatement to call it an operating theatre, but it wasn't quite a normal examination room either. It was small and windowless and chock-full of monitors and trolleys and oxygen cylinders. My eyes darted around it, trying to read the small print on pouches of liquids, hoping they knew their sedative from their saline. I'd been on high alert for weeks now, and my internet research had been so thorough that I was quite ready to take over at the slightest flicker of incompetence.

The sedative, when it finally kicked in, was miraculous. It made me feel almost like a normal human being – nervous, yes, but no longer quaking with fear. Maybe the music was helping too; I couldn't really say. I barely knew what I was listening to anyway. In fact it was only towards the end of the procedure, somewhere around the caecum, I'd hazard, that I noticed what had been playing.

My colonoscopy was being performed to the Hallelujah Chorus.

It's not unreasonable to be nervous about a colonoscopy. It would be pretty strange not to be, in fact. Even though my doctor had repeatedly used phrases like 'just a precaution' and 'highly unlikely' and 'almost certainly nothing', a colonoscopy is, if you'll excuse the expression, not to be sniffed at.

But I have to be honest with myself as well as you, and admit that I had gone way beyond reasonable anxiety and was two thirds down the path to Crazy Town. It's not *reasonable* to have spent the previous fortnight thinking about nothing but the tumour I was certain they would find. It's not reasonable to have woken every night sweating and sobbing and hyperventilating. And while it's perfectly reasonable to have a colonoscopy because you've experienced a sudden, dramatic loss of weight, it's *not* reasonable suddenly and dramatically to lose a lot of weight *because* you're having a colonoscopy. For two weeks, I'd felt so sick with worry that I couldn't eat more than a morsel of food without immediately wanting to throw it all up again. By the time I went in for the test, I was utterly convinced of the worst outcome. I was wondering whether history would be kind to me, whether I'd merit an obituary in any of the newspapers I occasionally write for, whether my kids would remember me fondly when I was gone. When I mentioned this to Phil, he suggested that if my final months were anything like the one we'd just had, everyone would be glad to be shot of me. Yes, it was harsh, but his point, I realised, was that most people don't react to precautionary medical investigations the way I do. Most people would wait until they've actually had a diagnosis of something awful before spiralling into despair.

So if all of the above *does* sound reasonable to you, then you might need to get some help. Because you, like me, suffer from health anxiety.

*

I'm a hypochondriac. There. I've said it. And actually that's quite a big deal, because in calling myself that I'm acknowledging the possibility that *some* of my fears about illness might be groundless.

Alcoholics often say that the hardest thing is to accept you have a problem. But for hypochondriacs, convinced as we are that all our symptoms are real, the hardest part is to accept you may NOT have a problem. In those weeks running up to the colonoscopy, I spent roughly 95 per cent of my time convinced I was fatally ill, and only 5 per cent entertaining the hope that it might not be anything serious. And the pernicious thing is that of course I might be ill, right now, as I type this. I could at any time have any number of life-threatening conditions. I will NEVER be sure that it's all in my head. So the trick is not letting that get to you. It's a trick I've never managed to master.

Some of my health scares seem ridiculous to me now. Like the lump on my foot, for example, which could of course have been malignant had it not had an utterly obvious and memorable cause. I'd been walking down a steep muddy slope and twisted my ankle. Before the slope my foot was lump-free. Immediately after, there it was, on the bit of my foot that was still sore from the twisting. So for the first day or so, I thought nothing of it. But when it was still there after a week, I began to think that it must be something more sinister. Perhaps it was some kind of tumour that had been there all along, and only the minor injury had revealed it. Or perhaps I hadn't stumbled at all, and had misremembered the whole thing. In which case, WHAT THE HELL WAS THIS LUMP DOING ON MY FOOT? I rubbed it and prodded it; I compared it with my other foot at night and in the morning. I imagined it aching in shoes that touched it, so I started to wear only those shoes that didn't. I prayed that it would simply disappear, and when it didn't I finally, reluctantly, called the doctor.

Now at our surgery, the receptionist will always ask if you're calling with an urgent problem. They don't need any more details than that – just 'Does this need to be dealt with today?' After weeks of putting off seeing a doctor, and searching the internet and the darkest corners of my imagination instead, by the time I'm desperate enough to call in a professional the answer is *always* yes. Yes, it *does* need to be dealt with today, because I know without a doubt that this time it's serious. And even if I'm wrong, I haven't slept or eaten properly for weeks, so that makes it urgent too.

But – and here's where things get complicated – because I'm English, I don't like to make a fuss. I don't want to jump the queue and be thought of as a time-waster or a troublemaker. My obsessive politeness trumps my obsessive worrying. So at that point, I'll frequently say 'No, it's not urgent enough to be dealt with today', and put myself – and those closest to me – through another few days of misery, as I pick at my food and trawl through ibetyouanymoneyitsterminal.com.

That's what I did with the foot-lump. There was enough self-awareness left in me to think that this probably was a fuss about nothing, so I agreed to an appointment for the following week, got off the phone and tried not to imagine people at my funeral saying, 'If only she'd gone to see about it sooner.'

The following day I was filming. I love filming when I'm going through a health-anxiety episode – it's the very best therapy there is. I have to concentrate on the job in hand, so it's wonderfully calming. I can't tell you how many times I've gone into work after a day or so of being too anxious to eat, and merely by virtue of having lines to remember and a costume to put on, found myself tucking into scrambled egg and mushrooms on toast without a second thought. It drives Phil crazy that I can't apply the same distraction techniques when I'm at home, but home – as I frequently explain to him – is where I'm truly relaxed, and it's only when I'm truly relaxed that I can allow myself to be tense.

So I was sitting on set during a break in filming, chatting to another actress, and because I was wearing high heels, I kicked them off for a moment. She glanced down as I did so, and casually remarked, 'What's that lump on your foot?'

'Oh, I twisted my ankle and I've had it ever since,' I said, trying to sound laissez-faire.

'How long?' she said, peering at it.

I could feel the panic welling inside me. I loosened my collar and mopped the sweat off my brow.

'Er . . . well . . . a few weeks. I suppose. Maybe a month.'

'You've seen a doctor, have you?'

It's an odd thing, but even though I spend all my time trying to convince Phil to take my 'symptoms' seriously, I don't want anyone else to. I'm not one of those hypochondriacs who wants doctors to scratch their heads and frown and refer me for tests. I crave an offhand shrug and a dismissive 'Oh *that*. That's *nothing*.' And I'm hoping for the same from anyone else I mention it to. I don't need drama – there's enough of that in my head already. It's reassurance I'm yearning for.

Anyway, my actress friend was resolutely refusing to

make me feel better. She stood up, marched over to the on-set medic and asked him to come and examine me.

Film sets can be treacherous places, so I don't want to diminish a medic's importance if an accident happens, but on an average day they mainly hand out plasters and paracetamol. This was by far the most exciting thing that had happened to him all week and he was damn well going to milk his moment in the spotlight. He put his glasses on and lifted my foot in both hands, holding it gingerly as if the lump might at any moment explode. He did all the things I'd been doing myself so obsessively – prodded it, rubbed it, compared it with the other one. And eventually he sucked in his breath and said, 'I'd get it looked ASAP if I were you.'

'What do you think it might be?' I asked.

'Well . . . hard to say . . .' he said.

'A sprain? Probably a sprain, right?'

'Might be,' he said.

'Or . . .?'

'Or . . . it might not. That's the trouble with lumps. You never know.'

That night I didn't wake in a cold panicky sweat, because I didn't get to sleep at all. So the next day I rang the doctor again and this time said it was urgent. I got an appointment for 11 a.m., but the morning seemed to drag interminably. I went for a walk, but all I could think about was the foot-lump. I came home, sat on the sofa and thought about it some more. By the time I got to the waiting room, it was a done deal as far as I was concerned. There would be a sharp intake of breath from the doctor, followed by the words 'referral', 'specialist' and 'tests'. My least favourite lexicon.

Then more internet searching, and more sleepless nights waiting for the test results which in turn would only provide more bad news.

When my name was called I walked into the surgery and started crying. She handed me a tissue and looked concerned. Please, I thought, please don't give me the concerned look.

'I'm sorry,' I began, 'I've got a problem with anxiety.'

'That's OK,' she said kindly. 'Then you've come to the right place. There are lots of ways we can help . . .'

'Oh no,' I explained. 'I'm not here about that. I'm here because I've got a lump.'

Her expression darkened.

'OK,' she said, 'well we can take a look at it and I'm sure it'll be nothing too serious. Whereabouts is the lump?'

'It's on my foot.'

'Your foot?'

'Yes. Sort of ankle-ish. I'll show you.'

I took off my shoe and sock and she bent down to take a closer look.

'I mean, I thought I'd twisted my ankle on a walk a few weeks ago, but now I'm thinking I may have imagined that. It's not right, though, is it? I mean, the other foot doesn't look like that. And the medic at work said I should get it checked ASAP because you can never tell with lumps. And . . .'

She'd straightened up by now, and I braced myself for the bad news.

'Yup. It's a ganglion,' she said, with unseemly breeziness.

'Right,' I whispered. I hadn't expected her to be able to say anything so definitive without a biopsy. But there it was.

A diagnosis. Not a sprain at all. A ganglion. Well, at least I'd found out quickly.

'Is there . . . anything you can do?'

'Well, in the old days we used to bash them with a Bible.'

'A Bible?' I repeated, wondering if this was some codified medical way of telling me to get praying.

'Or any big book,' she went on. 'In fact, I've got a medical dictionary here. I could have a go now, if you like –'

'Sorry,' I interrupted. 'I'm a bit confused. Are you saying –'

'I was joking.'

'Right,' I said. I remembered seeing medical student reviews years ago at the Edinburgh Festival. They were full of this sort of gallows humour. That's the trouble with doctors – they're nothing but grown-up medical students.

'So, is it . . . very serious?' I asked.

She looked puzzled.

'A ganglion? No. It's a harmless cyst. I'm so sorry, I would have explained that straight away, only the last time you came to see me I got the impression that you had medical training.'

Ah yes. Our last meeting. I couldn't remember what symptoms I'd presented with, but I do recall that when I used the phrase 'presented with' she suddenly started talking to me as if I were an expert. I wasn't trying to mislead her; it's a by-product of all the research I do that I pick up these little titbits. I'm the same with foreign languages – even though I can only speak basic French or Italian, my accent is convincing, so I sound as though I'm fluent.

'I don't have any training at all,' I said, feeling like I'd been caught out.

'Oh really?' she asked.

'Well, I do – as an actress. Although, to be honest, I don't even have much of that. It's just that I'm a hypochondriac and I google a lot. In fact, it's funny you mentioned medical dictionaries, because I used to have one myself, until my husband confiscated it.'

She didn't seem to think that was funny at all, which was fine because comedy's a subjective thing. But I couldn't help feeling she looked troubled, so I thought I'd put a positive spin on things.

'On the plus side, I always get the medical questions right on *University Challenge*,' I said.

It didn't seem to help.

'A ganglion isn't going to do you any harm at all,' she said calmly.

'Brilliant,' I said, and began gathering up my coat and bag.

'Trawling the internet for ill-informed medical "facts", however, *will*.'

She was right of course. And for the next few months I diligently avoided the medical websites. But the next 'symptom' that appeared, I was back clicking away. And it never ends well. Because even if I find the reassurance I'm seeking, I'll go on looking and looking. And sooner or later, I'll find a paragraph that begins: 'You should always consult a doctor, however, since in rare cases this can also be a symptom of . . . ' And I'm sucked right back into the vortex.

The colonoscopy was over, and I was still a little woozy from the sedative when the doctor came to give me his findings.

'So, basically,' he said, 'it was all fine. We took a couple of samples for analysis, but I couldn't see anything sinister. I don't think you've got anything to worry about.'

I felt elated. The weight of the entire world had been lifted from my shoulders. This feeling is, in my experience, one of the most pernicious things about hypochondria. You never feel quite as happy, skippy and life-affirmingly joyous as you do after convincing yourself you're dying and then being told you're not. Reassurance is a drug. You can get addicted to it. And the only way to get your fix is by really, really needing it. I'm not saying you consciously make yourself anxious and panicky in order to get that sense of euphoria. Not at all. But I'm saying it can make it harder to break the cycle, to get to the desired position of measured responses. And that, I know, is where I need to be. I need my worry to be measured, and my reassurance to be equally so. The one feeds the other.

That night, I ate a proper dinner and fell deeply asleep without tossing and turning and having to do relaxation exercises. When I woke at 3 a.m. and realised I didn't need to worry about it any more I felt elated all over again.

'We couldn't see anything sinister.' That's what he'd said. I lay there repeating it to myself. How funny, I thought, that throughout the whole process nobody had used the word 'cancer'. Not me, not the nurses, not the doctors – we'd all stuck resolutely to euphemisms. 'Nothing sinister', 'nothing to worry about', 'nothing too serious'. No one had ever said, 'We think you might have cancer.' Which meant, of course, that no one had actually said, 'We DON'T think you've got cancer.' In fact, now that I came to think about it, no one had actually told me explicitly that that's what they were looking for. So . . . was it possible . . . (and this is where the 3 a.m. thinking really kicked in) . . . that they didn't find 'anything serious' because they weren't looking for 'something serious'? Was it possible that there WAS in fact 'something serious' and it was still lurking there, undiscovered?

And that was it – there was no way I was going back to sleep.

I got out of bed, went downstairs and made a cup of tea. And on the off-chance that it might actually help this time, I put on some music to relax me.

DOLLY AND MILLIE TAKE TEA

'So what do you fancy?'

'A cup of tea'll be very nice.'

'Just tea?'

'Very nice.'

'What would you like with it?'

Auntie Millie gave the little half-smile that she always gave when she hadn't heard the question.

'She didn't hear you,' said my grandma. 'YOU DIDN'T HEAR HIM, DID YOU?' she shouted at her sister.

'It's OK, Mum,' Dad said, partly to stop her yelling in a public place and partly to avert a row.

'Very nice,' Millie repeated. She hadn't heard, but she was hoping that might be what the situation called for.

'HE'S ASKING IF YOU WANT ANYTHING TO EAT?' yelled Grandma, inches from Millie's head.

'It's fine, Mum,' Dad said. 'Let her look at the menu. I'll ask her in a minute.'

The tea shop was pleasantly characterless. There were glazed pine dressers full of flowery crockery, William Morris curtains, sugar tongs resting on a lace doily. It was all un-impeachably tasteful, and deathly quiet in the way that only an English tea room can be. We sat looking at the menu and Mum read a few items out loud. I think she wanted to make it look as though we were having a conversation like a normal family.

'Ooh, hot chocolate,' she said with awe, and did a sort of smack of her lips to convey how tempting this was. 'Scones and jam. Yummy.' You'd have thought she'd never encountered such riches. The waitress was hovering now, so Dad felt obliged to give Millie another try.

'Have something to eat, Auntie,' he said, projecting his voice as if to the upper circle. 'Something to go with your tea. A sandwich? A bit of cake?'

'A SCONE? YOU WANT A SCONE?' yelled Grandma. Her voice had become dry and rasping with age, but it could certainly travel. Millie looked at her uncertainly. 'SCONE,' Grandma bellowed.

'Yes, scone. I heard you,' Millie said with a frown. 'What about it?'

'YOU WANT ONE? CHARLIE'S OFFERING.'

The waitress smiled faintly at Dad, then slipped her pen back in her apron pocket and padded away.

'Let her have what she wants, Mum. It doesn't have to be a scone . . . '

'OR A SANDWICH? YOU WANT A SANDWICH?'

Millie looked at the menu again, and Grandma jabbed her finger at the list of sandwiches.

'CHEESE? EGG? THEY GOT SMOKED SALMON. YOU WANT A BIT OF SALMON? A SMOKED SALMON SANDWICH? OR A SCONE?'

Millie looked blankly at the menu, then at Grandma and finally allowed her gaze to settle on me and Jeremy. A smirk crept across her face, and with a cheeky nod towards her sister, she said at full volume but as if in confidence: 'She treats me like I'm potty.'

The visits to Auntie Millie were a twice-yearly treat for us. She was Grandma Dolly's younger sister, though in looks and temperament they were nothing like each other. Millie was grey-haired and rounded, and wore housecoats and flowery dresses, while Grandma was wiry and neat with dyed hair, lipstick and matching accessories.

Millie had moved away from London to Northampton when she got married before the war. She'd raised her family there and, now widowed, she lived alone in a narrow Victorian house. Unlike Grandma, who never encouraged visitors, Millie liked to entertain, and when we made the drive north, she'd always make sure her sons and their wives, girlfriends and children all piled in as well. She was a great baker of cakes and plates of Victoria sponge, cherry madeira and honey cake would teeter over the edge of the lace cloth, waiting for some overexcited child to knock them flying.

She'd been deaf for as long as I could remember, but as her sons often pointed out she heard everything she needed to. It never seemed to worry her; she would sit (if she sat at all) with a teacup on her lap and a beatific smile on her face, gazing at the rowdy, lively family she'd created.

Grandma was an altogether more brooding presence. For her, not only was the glass half empty, but the stuff you'd already drunk from it would more than likely poison you.

She couldn't get through the front door on a Friday evening without telling us which of her neighbours needed a hysterectomy. But to Auntie Millie, all news of her old London friends was welcome, so the two of them would sit for hours gossiping, and Millie lapped up every detail of who was sick or bankrupt or 'playing around'. I never fully grasped these titbits. Grandma would deliver the more salacious details in a throaty stage whisper which Millie could somehow hear and the rest of us, bizarrely, couldn't. And when a higher level of discretion was called for, the sisters would lapse into Yiddish.

'She's such a gute neshome,' Millie would say, and Grandma would nod sadly and add, 'She's better off without that gonif.'

There were three siblings in fact. The youngest, Lionel, was only rarely in touch with his sisters due to some perceived slight or ancient disagreement. I never understood what had caused it, because they didn't speak about it. Quite possibly they couldn't remember themselves. But when he made contact with one or other of them, they would share the details of his conversation thirstily, and since so much of the time they were together was spent talking about him, I often wondered why they didn't just invite him along. Love though couldn't completely erase resentment, so the sisters clung together in spite of age and geographical distance, each being the other's sole life-raft of memory. They wrote long letters in sloping copperplate, and Grandma would often read the salient bits out to us over Friday-night supper. Thus, in between visits, we kept up to date with one son's promotion and another's latest girlfriend, and when we were finally all in the same room, it would feel as if we'd never been apart.

For Jeremy and me, Millie was a firm favourite. She was mischievously funny, and often when she seemed to be gazing into silent nothingness with a gentle smile on her face, she was actually thinking up a barbed remark and waiting for her moment to strike. Sometimes you could make her laugh, if you said it loudly enough and enunciated very clearly, and she would be overcome with wheezy delight. It was usually Dad who had this effect on her. She'd wipe tears from her eyes, smack him on the arm and shout – since her deafness gave her little volume control – 'You silly sod!' And then Grandma would laugh too, reluctantly at first as though it was slightly undignified, but eventually as helplessly as her sister.

In fact my memories of those visits are characterised by laughter. I don't remember Dad ever being wittier than in Auntie Millie's dining room, with a slab of fruit cake in his hand, and Mum's pleas to 'calm down, Charlie, you'll choke yourself'.

This helpless hysteria took hold even on the day of Lionel's funeral. Millie and Grandma had never been to a crematorium before; Jews prefer to bury rather than burn. But Lionel was rebellious even in death, and while the eulogy was read in the featureless chapel, there they sat in their synagogue coats, grief-stricken and with who knows what remorseful or regretful thoughts crowding their heads. Millie reached into her bag to get a tissue, but when she had finished rootling around and looked up, the coffin had disappeared behind the curtain.

'Oh my GAWD,' she trumpeted, 'where's he gone?' And Dad, locked in a momentary battle between grief and laughter, gave in to the latter, taking the rest of the family with him.

It was only a short while after this that Millie was taken ill. Grandma waited anxiously for updates from the hospital, filling us in on the minutiae of the treatment and the food and the other patients on the ward, because talking about her sister kept her close by. And to her great relief and ours, Millie was out within a day or so with a clean bill of health, and we all piled into the car to go and see her.

Being Millie, she wanted to make us lunch, spend a whole day baking as she always did. But Mum and Dad were having none of it. Millie wasn't to lift a finger. We would take her out for once, a bit of a treat.

That's how we'd come to be in this suffocatingly quiet tea shop, failing to give our order.

Eventually Dad asked the waitress to bring us a selection of sandwiches and cakes and leave them in the middle of the table so everyone could help themselves.

At the other tables, people were exchanging awkward, hushed non sequiturs.

'The strawberry jam's lovely.'

'Delicious toasted teacakes.'

'Looks like it's clouding over.'

We didn't have that option. Millie wouldn't be able to join in unless we all shouted.

We talked a little about anodyne subjects – the weather, the traffic on the journey up to see her, where we were going on holiday. And then the food arrived.

'That all looks lovely,' Mum said, and shot a warning look at me and Jeremy to stop us grabbing the biggest eclair or the squidgiest slab of upside-down cake until Millie and Grandma had had first dibs.

'Help yourselves,' said Dad in his newly adopted Henry Irving baritone. 'Take whatever you fancy.'

Millie looked quizzically at the spread.

'Victoria sponge,' she observed.

'Yes,' hollered Dad. 'Go ahead.'

'How much did they charge you for that?'

Dad started to say that he didn't want her worrying about the bill, this was his treat; but Grandma still had hold of her menu.

'SEVENTY-FIVE PENCE A SLICE,' she yelled at her sister.

'How much?' Millie replied. She'd heard it all right; she just couldn't believe it. 'What a rip-off. They've got a nerve, these people . . .'

Mum glanced nervously around while Dad tried to pacify his aunt. But Grandma had the louder voice, and was busy pouring oil on the fire.

'TERRIBLE, ISN'T IT? WHAT THEY ONLY GET AWAY WITH!'

'Seventy-five pence, that's fifteen bob!' shouted Millie. '*I* make a nice Victoria sponge, don't I, Dolly? You like my sponge?'

'YOU MAKE A LOVELY BIT OF SPONGE. MOIST.'

'It *is* moist. It's very moist. Not like this. This is dry.'

Everybody was looking now, including the waitress, who lurked uncomfortably, wondering how a simple order had become so controversial.

'You know how much it costs me to make it? Charlie?'

Dad reiterated that the money wasn't important . . .

'WHAT IS IT, FLOUR, EGGS, A BIT OF JAM . . .?' Grandma chimed in, warming to Millie's theme. I hadn't seen them so absorbed by a subject since Cousin Ella had a goitre removed.

'A bit of flour and some eggs,' continued Millie. 'Butter, jam . . . it's nothing. It doesn't cost anything. Most of that you've got in the cupboard anyway. They've got a nerve, these people.'

It was a relentless assault. These two sisters, hewn from a childhood of hardship where if you had money at all you certainly you didn't throw it around, were exercising their right to be outraged. And thanks to age and infirmity they didn't give a damn who heard them.

You could feel embarrassed or horrified if you wanted to, and Mum unquestionably did. But there was only one thing you could actually *do* about it, and Dad went right ahead and did it. He laughed, at first surreptitiously, and then helplessly. Jeremy started laughing too, then me, and finally Grandma and Millie. I don't think anyone else found it·funny. I'm not even sure Mum did, worried as she must have been about someone choking to death on dry, over-priced cake. But the two old ladies laughed until they wept at the 'nerve of these people' and the fecklessness of the younger generation that they didn't know when they were being 'had'.

After Millie had hit Dad's arm, as we knew she would, and told him he was a 'silly sod', she wiped her eyes on a tissue from her bag and tried her best to compose herself. Then she bit into a slice of sponge and chewed it ruminatively for a minute. Only once she'd swallowed it and dabbed her mouth did she give a grudging shrug. 'The funny thing is,' she shouted, 'it's actually not that bad!'

Dad shot an apologetic smile at the waitress and asked for the bill.

MOTHER TONGUE

On my one day off in Vilnius, I had some people to meet. They were strangers who had no connection to my family or friends, but I still felt I had to meet them, because I knew they were just like me.

We used to laugh at my grandma's highly developed 'jewdar' – that unerring ability to spot a co-religionist a mile off. When Grandma saw, say, Lauren Bacall on the telly and whispered 'Yiddishe girl, you know?' it wasn't a value judgement. Bacall was no better or worse for being Jewish, but nevertheless it was something she and my grandma had in common.

Her generation were also attuned to the differences between groups of Jews – they could tell from a surname whether someone's antecedents were Sephardi (from Spain or Portugal), Mizrachi (from North Africa or the Middle East) or Ashkenazi, like us (from Germany, France or Eastern Europe). Indeed, even within these subgroups, I often heard Grandma divine whether someone was a Polak (Polish) or a Litvak (Lithuanian).

The Litvaks were always spoken of with a kind of awe. They were the brainy ones: the philosophers, scientists, political theorists, Talmudic scholars. I'm sure there were equally brilliant people in other parts of the diaspora, and some not-so-great minds in Vilnius. But if Grandma's hushed tones were anything to go by, this was a great community – both in number and in achievements.

When the Second World War came along, the Litvaks' brilliance was no match for the Nazis' brutality; 90 per cent of them were wiped out. Not just the sculptors and poets, physicists and mathematicians, but the butchers and barbers, teachers, grocers, friends, lovers, parents, grand-parents, children. Some were arbitrarily rounded up and shot. Others, duped into thinking their brains might save them, answered job advertisements for clerical work or accountancy. There were no jobs, or at least not for long, and they were killed too. All these people, thousands of them, were herded into ghettos, placed under dehumanis-ing strictures, and murdered on a whim. There were once 105 synagogues in Vilnius; now there was one, and hardly enough people to fill it.

So on my one day off, I couldn't in all conscience be a tourist; couldn't just wander through the old town eating cepelinai and buying linen tablecloths. I had to pay homage, remember strangers whose lives, but for the grace of God or a wrinkle in history, might have been mine. I had some people to meet.

The synagogue was closed that day, it turned out. I'd tried the museum of Jewish life, but that was closed too. So my only chance was the tiny Holocaust Museum, and so far no one was answering the door. If I'm totally honest, it would have been a relief to be able to say I'd done my best, and then go shopping. But I felt a duty to learn the history of the streets I'd been walking, so I tried the bell again, and this time, peering through the glass, I saw someone approaching.

A small, balding man opened the door and smiled at me.

'Come on in,' he said. He wasn't Lithuanian. A New Yorker, by the sound of him. I thanked him and started to step inside. But suddenly a woman came barrelling up behind him and stuck her arm across the doorway.

'You're not supposed to let people in, Harry,' she said.

'She's OK,' said Harry, as if I couldn't hear him. 'Look at her.'

'What, look?' said his wife. 'How can you tell?'

I wasn't offended. I could see her point.

Every year, at Passover, when Jews get together to read the festival prayer book or Haggadah, one of its gloomier lines jumps out at me:

'For not just one alone has risen up against us, but in every generation some have risen up to destroy us.'

This was after all a Holocaust museum; you couldn't blame her for being cautious.

'I was hoping to have a look around,' I said, trying to sound harmless.

'Sorry, honey,' said Harry's wife. 'It's just, you know . . .'

'Oh, of course,' I said.

'There's a sign.'

'Of course.'

'What sign?' said Harry, still smarting.

'On the door, Harry. Please do not admit other visitors. There. Right in front of your nose.'

From behind Harry and his wife, a tiny bird-like lady had now appeared. She crossed the lobby and, lifting a wooden flap in the counter, silently stepped inside the ticket booth. I pointed this out to them, thanked Harry for giving me the benefit of the doubt and went to buy a ticket.

This woman was Lithuanian. 'We have book guides,' she said as I bought my ticket, 'and there is tour if you like.'

I hate tour groups. It makes me tense when all the other people stand there and don't respond. I feel like I have to prove we're listening, and then I go too far, nodding and mouthing things like 'gosh' and 'crikey' and 'who knew?' Also I'm never sure whether you're supposed to clap at the end. So, I told her I'd rather look at things on my own.

'OK. That room first. There is big writing on wall.'

I went in and stood in front of a display panel, a board full of statistics and facts – how many Jews were living in Vilnius in the early 1930s, demographic breakdowns and numbers relative to the general population.

I'm not good at maths, so it was all a bit dizzying. I moved on to the pictures. School buildings and libraries and synagogues. Factories, offices and town squares. And faces. What drew me in were the faces of the people I'd come to see. Looking out from permits and identity cards, from sports teams and educational gatherings were all these faces who looked like people I knew. Almost all of those ordinary, complicated, full-of-life people would be dead within the next ten years. If only they'd been able to do what I was doing now, to read the writing on the wall.

In the next room, the tour party was being addressed.

I could hear an elderly woman speaking, I assumed, in Lithuanian, and a younger man translating for the American tour group. But I tried to screen it out. I wanted to be alone with these faces.

As the woman in the next room spoke, though, a phrase here or there jumped out at me as familiar. It was only maybe one word in fifty, but enough to puzzle me. If she'd been speaking Lithuanian I wouldn't have understood any of it.

And suddenly, even without seeing her or hearing her story translated, I knew one thing: the language she was speaking and these faces belonged together.

When my dad was a little boy, his grandmothers rarely spoke to him in English. They had both come to London some twenty years previously, but living in the East End, surrounded by co-religionists, even though some were Polish, some Russian, some Lithuanian, some Hungarian, they could get by perfectly well in Yiddish, the centuries-old lingua franca of the Ashkenazi Jews. Dad was born in the UK, as were his parents, so they all spoke English. But whenever he went to spend a day with one of the 'boobas' (grandmas), they would speak to him in their language and he would answer them in his.

One more generation on, and for my brother and me Yiddish was no longer a language; it was just a collection of words and phrases, much-loved relics that were already slipping from our grasp. What remained however was so ingrained in our vocabulary that we often forgot our non-Jewish friends wouldn't understand. To this day I find myself saying that I'm 'on spulkes' rather than tenterhooks, or that some self-proclaimed expert is 'a bit of a chochem', and it's only when I get a blank look back that I remember these are Yiddish phrases of which the rest of the world remains sadly deprived.

In our house, Yiddish was used chiefly when you wanted to abuse someone. The Inuits may have dozens of words for snow, but the Jews have an entire lexicon for idiocy. You might be a shmok or a shmendrik, a pots, a kvetch or a nar. But it wasn't only used as a weapon. There were certain phrases that had to be uttered to meet the demands of superstition. If you mentioned someone who'd died, you had to say 'olevasholem' (may they rest in peace). If you were leaving on a journey, you'd be told to 'geh, gezinta heit' (go in good health).

A criminal was a 'gonif', especially if he kicked you in the 'kishkes' (guts). A 'ferschtinkerner momzer' (stinking bastard) like that, you needed like a 'loch in kop' (hole in the head). But if your 'boychikle' (son) turned out to be a 'mensch' (good guy), there was no better language with which to 'kvell' (beam with pride) to your 'mishpochas' (relations).

The London suburb where I grew up had a substantial Jewish community. We were still very much in the minority – only a handful of my school friends were Jewish – but there were enough of us to have a network of synagogues, kosher butchers and delicatessens. One of these, Goldfarbs, was on my way home from school. While my friends went into the sweetshop for packets of Refreshers, or to the bakery for iced buns, I would take my pocket money and join the queue for olives. Everybody in Goldfarbs was English but they, like my parents, would slip into Yiddish when they felt that nothing else would quite do. So while I waited to be served, I'd let the chat wash over me. It made me feel warm and safe, I suppose. I knew I belonged.

Mr Goldfarb himself was usually out the back expertly slicing smoked salmon, calling through the hatch to one of the customers.

'How many ounces, Barbara?'

'Just give me four, Joe.'

'Four? Four's gurnisht.'

'I'm on a diet. I don't want to fress.'

Meanwhile, his wife would be taking orders for rye bread, onion pletzels and beigels. Nobody where we lived called them 'baygels'. That was what they said on American TV shows or if you were posh. We called them 'bye-gles', and even though if you say it like that in a sandwich shop people will think you've got it wrong, it still doesn't feel natural to me to pronounce the first syllable 'bay'. Let beigels be beigels, I say.

The Goldfarbs had an assistant called Lionel, who was in his fifties and had worked there since Old Mr Goldfarb first opened the shop. Lionel handled the deli counter – slicing wurst, spooning shmalz herrings and rollmops into little polystyrene tubs, along with pickled cucumbers, chopped liver and egg salad with onion. I'm actually salivating as I type this. Lionel had a lazy eye, which meant you could never be quite sure who he was serving. This was fine if I was with my parents, but sometimes, when I went in on my own, I'd answer a question that wasn't meant for me and be suffused with teenage embarrassment.

'No wurst today, Lionel. Bradley's got a new mishegoss.

Suddenly he's a vegetarian. Like I haven't got enough tsuruss.'

'Listen, zei gezunt. As long as you've all got your health,' he'd say. And then, 'Mum and Dad all right, bubbala?' I'd take a chance that that was aimed at me, and grunt a response, but in English – I wasn't confident I'd get it right in Yiddish.

At home though I used it with gusto, even though I only knew a handful of phrases. I'd use it for things for which there was no real translation, or which would have lost their potency in any other tongue. I'd use it to fit in, but also because it added a bit of colour and humour to whatever I was trying to say. But could I say I spoke Yiddish? No. Definitely not. I could have communicated better in Latin than in what my great-grandmothers would have called 'the mamma-loschen'. My family, like Joe Goldfarb and Barbara and Bradley and Lionel – we were modern Jews. English Jews. No one we knew actually spoke Yiddish any more. Why on earth would we need to? We'd assimilated.

A friend, who isn't Jewish, told me this story recently: his father was queuing up one day in a shop in Leeds, and an elderly Jewish man was in front of him. It was summer, everyone was wearing short sleeves, and my friend's dad happened to glance down and see a tattoo on the old man's arm. It was a faded grey collection of letters and numbers – the unmistakable mark of a concentration camp survivor. He was still looking at it and wondering what horrors he must have endured when the old man turned around and caught him.

'I'm so sorry,' said my friend's dad. 'I didn't mean to stare. It's just . . . seeing it like that . . . well, I was surprised.'

The old man gave a sardonic half-smile and raised his eyebrows.

'*You* were surprised?' he said.

The Jews of Vilnius would have been surprised too. After all those centuries, they must have felt like they'd assimilated – more than assimilated – like they *belonged*. But when it came to it, they were still outsiders. On one of the displays in the museum was a facsimile of a letter by the senior Nazi in charge of overseeing their fate. He was delighted, he told his superiors back in Germany, by the eagerness of so many locals to help with the rounding-up and the shootings and the burials in mass graves.

I don't know whether these people I'd come to meet, these faces, would have spoken to each other in Lithuanian or in Yiddish. Perhaps, like my family, they only used the mamma-loschen when they wanted to swear or order herrings. But this old lady addressing the tour group at the Holocaust Museum was speaking it now. Maybe she wanted to keep the language alive against all the odds. Or perhaps, like me, it made her feel warm and safe.

I realised I'd never heard fluent Yiddish before, only those bits and pieces I'd grown up with. It sounded familiar in its rhythms and cadences, but I barely understood a word. I moved closer to the group so that I could properly hear her. Harry's wife saw me, smiled and made a space for me.

'You gotta hear this story,' she whispered. 'It's incredible.'

And it was – a story of unimaginable tragedy, desperate

acts, heroism and humanity. On the day the Nazis finally decided to clear the Jewish ghetto (those streets through which I'd walked to come here), this woman had escaped by the simple fluke that they didn't spot the yellow star on her coat. She had run away and joined the Resistance, spending the rest of her war holed up in the woods, engaged in acts of sabotage.

Like everyone else in the group, I listened to the translation in awe. But when the interpretor wasn't speaking, I let the old lady's voice and that language wash over me.

At the end of it all, I wanted to speak to her, to thank her for bringing back to life the people I'd come here to meet. But I didn't know what to say. I couldn't even muster the Yiddish word for thank you – which was remarkable when you consider that I knew the words for three types of pickled cucumber and a dozen kinds of idiot. But even if I could, I didn't want to speak to her in Yiddish. It would have felt cheap, like I was making some tenuous bond between us. She'd lived a life I've only witnessed in films and nightmares, so even though she was Jewish, she was no more like me than my grandma was like Lauren Bacall. But as I waited for the crowd to disperse, she turned and saw me lurking, and I felt the sort of flush I used to feel when I wasn't sure if Lionel had asked me a question.

I stepped towards her and shook her hand in a very British way.

'It has been an honour to meet you,' I said. She smiled and nodded. And that was it. I made my way out, past the sign on the door advising against letting in strangers.

'In every generation some have risen up to destroy us.'

I went back outside and headed towards my hotel, past

the sites of synagogues that were no longer there and back through the picturesque old town streets. This time as I walked, I didn't just look at the architecture and the restaurant menus and the displays in linen shop windows. Instead I peered down alleys and through gateways and up towards higher floors. I thought about the people I'd sort of met and the woman who was keeping them alive. I tried to picture them living day-by-day, chatting in Lithuanian but cursing and joking in Yiddish. It was hard to understand how this beautiful place had become their prison and their grave, and I didn't want to dwell on that now. I preferred to think of it as it had been for centuries – as their home.

THE GIRL IN THE CAPE

In the winter of my fifteenth year, I decided to wear a cape. It wasn't a poncho or a shawl or a Margaret Rutherford-style tartan affair. I wasn't wearing it as fancy dress or for a bet. It was my everyday winter coat – a long, brown cape made of heavy felted wool – and I loved it.

Many years later, when I told my children about the cape, they were strangely unsurprised. The idea of me as a child has always seemed ridiculous to them, because from everything they've heard I was so unchildlike.

A neighbour remarked to my mum when I was five years old that talking to me was like talking to a little old woman. Mum told me because she thought it was funny, but actually that's how I thought of myself too. You know those early Renaissance paintings of the Madonna and child where the baby looks like an elderly man? Well, in my head that was me as an infant – without the halo, of course, but with the strangely wizened, disturbing precocity. I wasn't unusually clever, nor even emotionally mature. But I felt and seemed older than my years, somewhat world-weary and set in my ways. I had lots of friends, but I don't think I ever truly belonged with other children. I was just visiting, with one ear on what the grown-ups were talking about. I liked what they liked – black-and-white films, classical music, Ella Fitzgerald, Pre-Raphaelite paintings, and stories of young women on windswept moors.

My own children, by contrast, are utterly of their time. They're literate in popular culture, know their way round social media, dress fashionably, use the right slang in the right context. They seem, as far as I can tell, to have interior lives that are age appropriate. They fit in.

I don't regret being different. I was a very happy child most of the time, so it didn't cause me any problems. In some ways, I'm rather proud of it – I was my own person, and managed to get along nicely. But there were other kids, cooler, more fashionable, more relaxed in themselves, who I admired and aspired to be like, and when I look at my son and daughter I see the reflection of those kids, not of me.

For Ollie and Tilly, this image of their mother as a teenager in a cape is an irresistible comedy gift. Whenever I mention, as mothers do, that *I* never did this or that when *I* was their age they can say, 'No, but on the other hand . . . you wore a cape.' On one occasion, when I was talking to them about my closest group of school friends, and Ollie referred to them wryly as 'the cape clique', I felt I had to set the record straight. They weren't *all* wearing capes, I explained. If he imagined that it was some kind of tribal signifier, then he was very much mistaken. It was just me, flying the flag for individuality, showing my willingness to stand out from the crowd.

But the more I tried to explain it to him, the harder it

became to explain it to myself. I had never previously dressed to be noticed. My other clothes at the time were distinctly . . . undistinctive. The cape was an anomaly, and I couldn't help feeling there must have been more to my wearing it than met the eye.

For one thing I can't remember buying it. Since I didn't have money of my own, one of my parents must have been with me at the time, but when I asked them, they both denied it – a little too vehemently, now I come to think of it.

Mum has always been fashion conscious. She grew up gorgeous and blonde in the fifties, so for her clothes were about jewel colours, satin stilettos, hooped petticoats, long gloves and scarves. To this day she holds as sacrosanct the importance of a matching accessory. In my late teens and twenties, when I'd ditched the cape and started going out for the evening in conventional attire, she would always notice if my shoes didn't match my bag. She'd stand at the top of the stairs and say, 'You look lovely . . . but I have got a scarf that's the *same* shade of grey if you want it.'

So I can't have bought the cape on her watch. She'd never have allowed it, and I'm amazed with hindsight that she didn't stage some kind of an intervention.

Dad, in his own way, was equally prescriptive about clothes. He followed a strict set of rules that I never understood governing when you should wear a double-breasted jacket and what kind of tie knot went with what kind of collar. But unlike Mum, he didn't care too much what *I* wore, as long as it kept me warm and dry. Dad lives in a heightened state of weather-preparedness. Back when Mum was worrying whether my scarf was slate-grey or dove-grey, Dad wanted me to replace it with a knitted one. Indeed, he rarely even called a scarf a scarf, preferring instead the word 'muffler', which was already so archaic in the seventies that I don't remember anyone else using it. I think he preferred it because it better conveyed that the point of this item was function, not fashion. A silk scarf was a thing of beauty, but it wouldn't stop you getting pneumonia. No matter how smartly dressed I was, Dad would always plead with me to take a muffler and a cagoule. In fact, throughout my childhood I only remember two major arguments with my dad, and both involved me not wanting to wear a waterproof.

So it must have been Dad who let me buy the cape.

But the other mystery is where on earth we bought it from. I can't emphasise this strongly enough – capes were very much not in fashion at the time. We couldn't afford to buy fancy designer gear, so somehow I must have found this thing in C&A or the local department store. But no fashion buyer would have bought in a stock of the things, unless they'd got wind of a Franciscan monastery opening up nearby.

However I'd come to be in possession of the cape, I was immensely proud of it.

I liked the way it swung out at the sides when I walked fast, and the fact that on cold days I could hide my hands inside. It suited me perfectly. It was, apart from anything else, a bang-on match for my hair, which was also long and brown with the texture of felted wool. But more than anything, I loved it because no one else had one. It slightly surprised me that they didn't, what with the swinginess and the cold-weather-hand-hiding thing. If it had ever become a trend though, I knew I'd have to ditch it, since so much of its appeal was uniqueness.

There's a very thin dividing line between weird and mysterious, and for me the cape fell on the right side of it. I didn't want to be an oddball, but I did want to look dramatic. I've been trying to remember if some cultural allusion had prompted this, and the only thing I can think of is that I had, around that time, watched an early Dracula film starring Bela Lugosi, and been terribly struck by the leading man. He seemed a personable kind of a vampire, a bloodsucker you could do business with. Indeed, I recall now that I had a picture of Lugosi on my bedroom wall. But before you judge me, remember that the next generation of teens were obsessed with the *Twilight* films.

Anyway, whatever had prompted it, I knew in my heart that when I wore the cape I cut quite the dash. As I strode between school and home, it billowed about me commandingly. Some passers-by might have thought they'd seen a short girl wrapped in a blanket, but in fact they'd witnessed a vision, a wonder, an enigma.

It became something of a talking point, which I took to be a good thing, and because nobody mocked me about it to my face, it didn't occur to me that they were probably doing so as soon as I turned my back.

Even in the school staffroom the cape was a subject of discussion. I found this out one day after class when my music teacher asked if he might have a quiet word. He told me, in a hushed voice, that he too had a cape, though, he added hastily, he *very* rarely wore it. In his spare time he was a harpsichord player, and his mother had made him an opera cape to wear over his tailcoat for concerts. But he didn't feel – and here I was conscious he was choosing his words carefully – that an opera cape was quite his thing. It would take a greater degree of confidence than he possessed to carry it off. I didn't argue with him – I could see that if you spent the rest of your days wearing brown tweed jackets with leather patches on the elbows it might be a leap too far. Anyway, he'd been wondering what to do with it and he thought perhaps I'd like to have it, to add to what he assumed must be my collection. I protested and said he couldn't possibly give away something his mother had lovingly toiled over. But I almost got the feeling he couldn't wait to be shot of it.

A few days later he brought it in for me and I waited until I'd got it home before trying it on. It was much more ostentatious than my monastic original; shorter, for a start, and midnight blue with a frankly startling lining of turquoise satin. And unlike my other one, which fastened with two rather dull brown buttons, this one had the glorious adornment of a silver chain with a fabulous lion-head clasp. I could see why he hadn't had the nerve to wear it. But I could also see the appeal of having a selection of capes for different weather conditions, social events, that sort of thing. I hung it lovingly next to my brown one in the cupboard under the stairs, and went to bed thinking I had everything a girl could want.

The next morning when I went to put it on, though, I almost lost my nerve. I showed it to my mum, who was less than reassuring. 'Well, it's . . . you know . . . dressier than the other one. I don't know. Is it the sort of thing your friends are wearing?'

It was most assuredly not the sort of thing my friends were wearing, which was of course the point. And ultimately it was this that persuaded me to give it a go.

So I set off for school looking like a Vatican guard.

It wasn't quite as swingy as my brown one, and being shorter, it didn't hide my hands either. Also I noticed it was scratchy around the neck. I fiddled with it, loosened it and untied it altogether. But the shiny lining made it slippery to wear unfastened, so I did it back up again, and completed the journey with my fingers inside the collar to stop it chafing.

I got to school and took it off, and realised the teacher's mum had left a pin in it. I removed it and hung the cape up on my hook in the cloakroom – it looked bizarrely out of place next to all the duffel coats, as though the Phantom of the Opera were paying a visit.

Several teachers that morning asked me if I was OK. Problems with schoolwork? Family all well? Friends seemed concerned about me too and I couldn't fathom why. It was only when I looked in the mirror at break-time that I understood: the pin had raised a large red welt on my neck. It was odd enough being the owner of a cape, odder still that I now had a second one, and perhaps even odder (though completely innocent) that the latter had been given to me by a young male teacher. But now it looked like I'd tried to slit my own throat, and that was an oddity too far.

I didn't wear the opera cape after that. But I stuck with my old faithful brown one for a good while longer.

What finally did for it was the skinheads. There was a

rowdy group of them in the year below mine who would hang around the baker's in the High Street after school, smoking and swigging beer. I wouldn't call it bullying. They'd just yell, with scant imagination but undeniable accuracy, 'You're wearing a fucking cape.' And after leaving it a few weeks to give the impression I didn't care, I finally caved in and stopped wearing it. I told myself it was nearly springtime anyway, but really I didn't need the hassle.

At least, I thought that was the reason. But I now I wonder if, in fact, I no longer needed the cape.

What was it about me, at that time, that made wearing it so appealing?

I asked Tilly why a girl of her age might wear such a thing, and after confidently stating that NO girl of her age would, she came up with a more nuanced answer. She said that if you were the kind of kid who wanted to look fashionable, but feared getting it wrong, then you might feel safer cocking a snook at fashion altogether. She didn't actually say 'cocking a snook', come to think of it, that was my phrase – I may no longer wear archaic garments, but archaic phrases are harder to shrug off. But I think she had a point. Certainly at that age I didn't understand how to look cool and I knew enough to realise that I'd never get it right if I tried.

But I think there were deeper reasons too. While the cape was getting me noticed, it was also covering me up. The one constant with every teenager I've ever met is embarrassment. You're embarrassed about your awkwardness and your lack of confidence; embarrassed by what you don't know and by what you're beginning to find out; and more than anything, you're embarrassed by your body. Young women in particular are endlessly judged and scrutinised. Strangers in the street shout comments about your breasts and your bum and your legs.

The cape protected me from all that. It was my invisibility cloak, my cocoon; a chrysalis that allowed me, for a few months at least, to do my growing-up away from prying eyes. It might have looked ridiculous, but it made a statement about who I was that didn't depend on the shape of my body. It hid me from the threatening gaze of the world.

For that one winter I felt dramatic, unafraid, unmissable and yet invisible. I was an ordinary kid and a harmless oddball. At a point in my life when I didn't know who I was, I briefly had an identity – I was the girl in the cape.

NOT A STORY

'So, where are you from?'

Phil and I were sitting outside a bar in a remote Italian town, enjoying a drink as the sun went down. I'd noticed the man at the next table trying to get our attention and was trying to tell Phil, through body language alone, that I wasn't in the mood for a chat. Don't get me wrong – I find people endlessly fascinating; I just don't feel the need to talk to them. I'd rather eavesdrop, get to know them by stealth. Shifty, I know, and don't think I don't feel guilty about it. But my defence is this: I meet new people every day of my working life. I chat to them, make small talk, ask them about their partners, their kids, their background – it's lovely and I wouldn't have it any other way. But on holiday, I need a break. So there I sat with crossed legs, a twisted torso, a hand up to my face and my chair turned inwards in a perfect dumb show of 'please don't come over and talk to me'. But Phil either failed to pick up on my signals or resolutely chose to ignore them. More likely the latter. It annoys him when I'm antisocial.

Before he met me, Phil travelled the world, usually alone, and quickly realised that if he didn't start conversations with the people he met along the way he would have a pretty miserable time of it. The habit stuck, and as the years passed this whole 'chatting to strangers' thing became a contentious issue between us, because while I recognised that it was a terrific survival skill for the lonely traveller, he wasn't alone now. He was with me, his antisocial wife. I was sitting right opposite him at every restaurant table, listening in to the couple next to us. Surely that was company enough. But he can't help himself. I've lost count of the number of times Phil's disappeared on a beach or a country path and come back half an hour later with a new friend. He starts by asking them if they know a good restaurant or pub, and before you know it he's arranged for us all to meet there. And I am forced to get to know these people, not by pretending to read and tuning in to their private conversations, but by being open, amiable and friendly. Like a decent human being, as he puts it. The bastard. It's probably grounds for divorce, now I come to think about it.

So outside the bar, while I was hunched over my drink in attempted isolationism, Phil was leaning back in his seat, making eye contact and smiling blithely at the world, casting his net to catch a friend.

And the guy at the next table bit.

He told us his name was Jacopo, and we told him our names too – well, Phil did. I sort of grunted. He asked if we were English and we said we were. From London? Yes. He knew London well. Friends in Ealing. Did we know Ealing? Not really. We should go there; it's nice, Ealing. Leafy.

I knew at once, with an awful certainty, that a few months from now we'd be having dinner in some Ealing trattoria with this man we'd spoken to once and his friends whom we'd never met. I glowered at Phil, and wondered if couple's therapy might not be a bad idea.

But he was in the swing of it now, oozing gregarious charm. It wasn't even small talk – a quick chat about the weather would have been bearable. But Phil likes to draw his subjects out. He'll ask a leading question, like 'I bet you've seen a lot of changes round here in your time, haven't you?' and then sit back and let them talk. And it's great in one way, to hear a new perspective, unique experiences. But it's also great sometimes to just . . . you know . . . talk to your wife.

I decided to stop fighting it – I was starting to irritate myself by being sour and tight-lipped. So I sat back in my seat and let it all wash over me. And inevitably, I got drawn in.

Jacopo told us that he had been born and brought up in this quiet town. He came here for a month every summer to visit his elderly mother who still lived in the same apartment he'd grown up in. But he now lived in Wiltshire, which accounted for the fact that his English was near-perfect and unaccented, and a damn sight better than our Italian.

'And what took you to England in the first place, Jacopo?' Phil asked.

Jacopo gazed off into the distance as if watching his past on a cinema screen.

'A woman,' he said at last, and it occurred to me that maybe this was going to be intriguing after all. Phil read my thoughts and shot me a smile that I can only describe as smug. Forget the new-friend thing – this I-told-you-so attitude was the first thing I'd mention in therapy.

We both sipped our drinks and waited for Jacopo to elaborate.

'She wanted to marry me,' he continued, 'but we were too young. Much too young. I said to her, you must be crazy!'

Phil looked at me again, and I couldn't resist a coy smile back, as if Jacopo's story mirrored the beginnings of our own romance. It didn't at all though, because we hadn't fallen in love as feckless teens in a Puglian hilltop village, but as adults at work who had waited ten years before getting married. Still, Jacopo was bringing out the romantic in us, which was progress considering moments earlier I'd been thinking of calling Relate.

He seemed to be aware of the effect he was having, and decided to take his time and enjoy himself. He sat back, took a slug of his beer and waited until he was good and ready to tell us more.

'Anyway, it turned out she was.'

'She was what?' I asked.

'Crazy,' said Jacopo.

'Crazy in love?' I ventured.

'No. Crazy. Mentally unstable. Not right in the head,' Jacopo said, with what I couldn't help feeling was a lack of compassion. 'And eventually, I went to England.'

'So you didn't go to England *for* a woman; you went to get *away* from one,' Phil said, by way of clarification.

'Yes,' said Jacopo. But then the romantic glint crept back into his eye. 'Only she followed me. It was a village in the middle of Wiltshire, and still she tracked me down.'

I had a picture in my head now of this young, shy, Italian boy and his too-hot-to-handle girlfriend. Surely at this point in the story he realised they were meant to be together.

Phil too was hoping there'd be a happy ending.

'And what happened?' he asked.

Jacopo took a final swig of his Peroni. 'Oh,' he said with a dismissive shrug, 'I sent her home again. I mean, I was seeing someone else. I never asked her to come all that way. And . . . you know . . .' and he did a whirly motion with his hand at the side of his head, 'she was cuckoo.'

For a moment, Phil and I sat in stunned silence, looking at the table. We felt cheated. Eventually, I spoke for both of us.

'I have to be honest, Jacopo, that's not the story I wanted to hear.'

Jacopo shrugged and gestured to the waiter to bring him his bill.

'But it's not a story,' he said in the same eminently reasonable tone as before. 'It's life.'

For a while after Jacopo left, Phil and I sat in the square sipping our drinks and thoughtfully nibbling olives. I couldn't get the 'crazy' girlfriend out of my head. Maybe she still lived here – could that be her on that bench in the piazza? Did she marry someone else? Have a family? A career? A life without Jacopo? Or was she still obsessed with him, crushed by the misfortune of unrequited love? Saving coins in an enormous jar to pay for a one-way air fare to Wiltshire?

Phil looked at me and grinned.

'You never want to meet new people,' he said, 'and then when you do, you can't stop going on about them.'

'I'll admit, he was interesting . . .' I said grudgingly.

'They're always interesting,' Phil said. 'You know that. That's why you eavesdrop on other people's conversations all the time instead of talking to me. But you never think of starting a conversation yourself. That's always got to be my job.'

'I just think it looks a bit needy. "Be my friend, talk to me." Like we can't survive without all these random strangers.'

'You probably can't,' Phil retorted. 'I bet you'll end up writing about Jacopo in one of your books, and I still won't get any thanks.'

'Now you're being ridiculous,' I said.

On the wall above the table where Jacopo had been sitting was a large marble plaque, the town's war memorial. I'd looked at it many times before and now my eye was drawn to it again.

It was a monument to the unknown soldiers – '*del milite ignoto*': those who had left this tiny place to fight for a cause they probably knew little about, and whose names had been lost over time. But as I looked at it, I noticed something odd. In the word '*ignoto*' the letter 'n' was carved backwards. It was in the words '*giorno*' and '*in*' as well, only in both of those it had been corrected, with an additional diagonal going the correct way, so that both words seemed to have a jaunty bow tie carved into them. It didn't matter in the least, of course, except that it drew me in in much the same way as a partially heard conversation at a neighbouring table would have done. I started to wonder about it, to want to fill in the gaps.

By now, Phil had noticed it too, so we paid for our drinks and went to take a closer look.

It was a large slab of stone, possibly marble – I couldn't tell since it was so far above my head – and carved with simplicity and restraint. Its position at the main entrance to the square added to its importance. You could picture the civic pride at its unveiling, and before that the meetings: who would design it, how much could the town afford and who should be commissioned to carve it?

We started to imagine the scene in the stonemason's workshop when he first spotted what he'd done wrong. Perhaps his wife had brought him in some bread and pro-sciutto, a flask of rough wine maybe, or some coffee. We were warming to our theme now. We could imagine the room – it would have been in one of the side streets off the square, that one over there perhaps. It would be cold and covered in dust from the carving and the smoothing and the . . . grinding? Neither of us knew anything about stonemasonry, so we moved on to the people instead. We knew about people. The mason himself would be buffing the finished monument with a cloth (Phil said a brush, but I wasn't sure that was technically accurate) when his wife . . . Maria, I suggested . . . came in:

Maria: You need a break, Beppe, you've been at it all day again.

Beppe: I'm stopping, I'm stopping. I think I've actually finished.

Maria: You have? That's terrific . . .

(Phil: Would she say 'terrific'?

Me: They're speaking Italian. The whole thing's in translation. I'm just trying to create an impression . . . Can we carry on now?)

Maria: That's terrific. I'm so proud of you, Beppe. Come and have your lunch.

Beppe: Take a look . . .

Maria: In a minute. Let me pour the coffee.

(Beppe stares at his handiwork)

Beppe: This is big, you know.

Maria: It's the biggest slab the council could afford.

Beppe: No, I mean for me. This is big for me. My most important commission to date.

(Maria walks over to Beppe and puts her arm around him.)

Maria: And they asked you first.

Beppe: We don't know that, Maria.

Maria: *I* know. If they'd asked Francesco, his wife would've told me.

Beppe: Well, maybe . . .

Maria: Not 'maybe'. I'm telling you. She loves rubbing my nose in how well her husband's doing. If Francesco had been offered it, I'd know. No. They asked you, Beppe. You're in the big league now. You've arrived.

(Beppe sips his coffee and puts a slice of prosciutto in his mouth. Maria looks at the carving. An uneasy silence.)

Beppe: Well?

(Maria doesn't speak.)

Beppe: Maria? Is it OK?

Maria: (uncertainly) It's terrific.

Beppe: You sure?

Maria: I'm sure. Terrific.

Beppe: I went for a sans serif font. I think it's classier. And once you start with the serifs, it's hard to know where to stop. Serifs here, serifs there . . .

Maria: Beppe, pass me my glasses . . .

Beppe: What? What's wrong? You think there should be serifs? I could serif it up a bit . . .

Maria: No. No. I like it better . . . sans. Beppe, you re-member that problem you once had with the letter 'n'?

Beppe: Of course I remember. The gravestone for Nico Nannetti, mourned by his wife, Nella, and their sons Niccolo, Nardo and Nunzio. Nine 'n's. I got five of them right, for crying out loud, but still they gave the next commission to that bastard Francesco. I won't make that mistake again.

Maria: Yes. Beppe . . . you might need a glass of wine.

By now, Phil and I had left the town square and climbed the hill to the restaurant. But even as we looked at the menu and got stuck into our antipasti, we were thinking about Beppe and Maria. At what point did Beppe hit upon the notion of reversing the slope in the 'n's? Of turning them into those butterfly shapes? Farfalle, he would have called them. It was one of the few Italian words we knew, on account of it being a type of pasta. And did he come clean straight away with the local dignitaries? Or did he and Maria try to brazen it out. 'What do you mean? There's nothing wrong with the "n"s. It's Beppe's trademark. It's a flourish. A new kind of serif. None of the other towns has a war memorial like it – that's what makes it special.'

And it was true, of course. It was what made it special. How many war memorials had we passed in our lives, both on holiday and at home? And how often had we given them more than a passing glance? It was shameful to admit it, but normally we'd slow down, maybe read a couple of the names, and then move on. This one had occupied our attention for the better part of an evening.

'But for all the wrong reasons,' I pointed out. 'Because we've turned its creation into a soap opera. A little domestic comedy. We're only interested in it because it's flawed.'

'But that's why it's brilliant. The people it represents were flawed too,' said Phil. 'Just because they died a horrible death far from home, doesn't mean they were perfect.'

And it struck me that he was right. A war memorial impeccably carved on pristine Carrara marble is a thing of nobility and dignity. But it's also cold and aloof and impersonal. The soldiers it represents, though – and after so many years they were *all* unknown warriors to us now – those young men were real. They were flesh and blood and bone, ordinary young men with dreams and frustrations. Men who wanted to be farmers or shopkeepers or – yes – stonemasons. Men who wanted to fall in love and have sex and marry. And maybe they ran away from the women who loved them, like Jacopo did. Or perhaps, given the chance, they would have stayed with them, had a family, created a home, like me and Phil. If they'd lived, they would have sat in that square where we'd sat, sipping drinks, having a row because one wanted to sit quietly while the other wanted to make new friends.

But they never got the chance to do any of that. Their lives were cut short by the horrible generality of war. Any young men would have served the purpose, but it happened to be them, their generation, taken far, far away from this quiet, beautiful town and shot at. They died too soon, but it doesn't make them saints and we do them no favours by pretending that it does. Better, surely, to think of them as ordinary boys, as real people.

After dinner, we went down to the square once more to look up at it, and this time we didn't think about Beppe and Maria. We thought about the boys, those lost souls, and the plaque that – quite accidentally – told their story.

Only Jacopo was right – it wasn't a story. It was life.

LET'S PRETEND

It had been, as ever, an interminable drive. Roadworks and hold-ups and wrong turns. I hated this journey, hated the fact that South London was still, after so long, unfamiliar territory. This is my city – I was born here, I've lived here all my life – but when I cross the river, I'm utterly baffled. I have no idea where Clapham is in relation to Vauxhall or Peckham or Herne Hill. None. So each time I made this trip, I had to stick rigidly to the route Phil had drawn out for me on a piece of scrap paper years earlier. Because if I strayed from it, I feared I may never see my home again.

But that wasn't all that was on my mind. I was miserable because I knew how relentlessly bleak it would be when I got there. Not South London – although now I came to think about it . . . no, not South London. I couldn't blame it on random geographical prejudice. It was the place I was going to that filled me with dread. The reception desk, the corridor, the day-room. The jaunty, pastel-and-beigeness of it all. The easy-to-wipe bright and breeziness. Apricot walls and grip handles and alarm strings hanging from ceilings.

Some days it was depressing in a memento mori kind of a way; because it reminded me that this could happen to me, to Phil, to any of us. In fact it probably will. If we don't keel over in an instant with a massive coronary or die a horrible, lingering, agonised, slow death, then we'll end up in a place like this: struggling to hold on to the vestiges of who we once were, eking out our remaining years in custard creams and episodes of *Cash in the Attic*. But sometimes it was depressing because coming here seemed so pointless. She wouldn't know who I was. She wouldn't know I'd been to see her. She wouldn't know I'd left. So who was this for? This miserable crawl through London traffic; this venture into the void – who was it actually for?

I pulled up in one of the visitors' bays and switched off the engine. Not yet. I couldn't go inside yet. I took a few deep breaths, inhaling – while I still had the chance – proper air full of exhaust fumes, not disinfectant and urine. I checked my face in the rear-view mirror. OK, maybe she wouldn't know it was *my* face, but she'd see *a* face, somebody sitting in front of her. It may as well be presentable. I got out my make-up bag and brightened up my blusher. 'Let her paint an inch thick, to this favour she must come.' Oh for crying out loud, let's get this over with.

Auntie Vera wasn't a real auntie, but I'd known her since I was a child, when 'auntie' was an honorific title given to anyone your parents brought you into contact with. We'd never been especially close, but I liked her – liked who she used to be, that is, since the 'her' in question wasn't really there any more. She was a strong woman who'd been through a lot and come out of it all remarkably unscathed. Before this cloud descended on her, this fog that was slowly engulfing her and causing the real 'her' to disappear, I used to pop in for a cup of tea and a catch-up whenever I was in the area. I'd listen to her stories – the same stories pretty well every time, admittedly, but a good yarn bears repetition. And these were extraordinary. At least, to my ears they were, but to anyone of her generation, they were commonplace tales of cruelty and contempt; of harsh treatment from people who should have been kind, and kindness from people who had nothing else to offer.

She'd had a miserable childhood. Her mother didn't want her and her father never knew she existed. So she was passed from household to household, to whoever could afford to look after her or felt that another pair of hands around the place might be useful. Sometimes she was neglected and abused. And sometimes she was given a tantalising glimpse of what life in a family could be – enough of a template for her to model her future on. So the stories, however often repeated, were never dull. She had a knack of bringing them to life, and you felt as though you knew the aunts and the uncles, the houses and the factories, the schools and the air-raid shelters.

Most of all, she liked to talk about her cousins. For a couple of years in her early teens, she had gone to live with Auntie Alice and Uncle Bert in a two-up, two-down in Twickenham. They had five children of their own, so money was tight. But somehow they managed to feed an extra mouth, and for the first and only time in her life (until she had a home and a family of her own, that is) Vera had felt she belonged. I don't know if these stories stuck in my head because she told them more often than the others, or because they were such a relief from the relentless miseries and indignities of everything else about her childhood. The neighbour who 'looked after her' when she was tiny, and whose idea of discipline was to sit little Vera on the hot kitchen range and burn the backs of her legs. The aunt she was first 'packed off to live with', who made her feel like an outcast and only gave her food once her own children had had first dibs. And her mother, who finally took Vera back in when she was of an age to earn a living, and pocketed almost every penny she brought home. To me these were horror stories; to Vera, they were life. Everyday unpleasantnesses from which the year or so with Auntie Alice was a shining respite.

At Alice and Bert's she'd had Rose, a cousin of her own age, to walk to school with. And there was Walter, the toddler – curly-haired, chubby, mischievous. Meals were haphazard, you had to get in quick as there wasn't enough bread to go round. But there was laughter and respect and affection. And it lasted just long enough for Vera to figure out that she wanted more of all those things.

And then Auntie Alice got ill and died. Vera never found out what was wrong with her, nobody talked about it. But Uncle Bert couldn't cope with it all on his own, so Vera was sent away, but worse even than that – the entire family was broken up. The older children went into service, and the younger ones? Vera never knew what happened to them. She herself went back to the horrible aunt and bitterly resented what had been taken away from her. But she was an optimist. She came through it all, married a good man, raised a family and modelled it on the one she'd fleetingly enjoyed.

There was one thing she couldn't get over though – she never saw Rose or Walter again.

'I still can't understand it,' she would always say at the end of the story. 'How could Albert let that little boy go?' I'd say that he sounded like a good man who had no choice, and she'd shake her head and murmur, 'But Walter was the loveliest mite.' And that would be my cue to go and put the kettle on.

The stories were long gone now. They were the last things to fade, staying alive far longer than the memories of what she'd had for lunch or whether she'd taken her blood-pressure pills. But now they too were tangled up with the fear and bewilderment that clouded her head. She had family who would visit, children and grandchildren, but not many and not often. So it didn't feel right to stop coming, even though she had no idea who I was when I did.

I pressed the security buzzer and waited for someone to let me in, downing a last gasp of fresh air in the meantime. After a moment, a carer appeared through the glass, checked my identity with a few cursory questions and showed me through to the day-room.

'How's she been?' I asked.

'Oh, she has her good days and her bad days,' was the reply, and I guessed that they said that about everyone.

'And which is it today?'

She didn't answer, but opened the door and waved me towards the farthest corner.

At first I didn't recognise Vera. They'd cut her hair – rather nicely as it happens – but it was hanging straight and flat and grey and not at all like the bouncy golden perm she used to have. She was asleep in a high-backed vinyl armchair, and a cup of tea with a wrinkled skin on top was cooling on the table next to her.

I went closer and peered at her, in case her head had just lolled and she was awake after all. Or perhaps in case she'd quietly slipped away. Would that be so terrible? Last time I visited it was what she was wishing for, all she kept saying again and again: 'I wish I was dead. Why am I still here?'

She was breathing shallowly, which was something of a relief to me if not to her.

I didn't want to stand here leaning over her. I tried to pull up another armchair, but it was heavy and I felt ridiculous dragging large items of furniture around. So I sidled over to the dining area, trying to look non-threatening and like I belonged. I took a smaller chair and headed back towards where Vera was slumped.

'Can I help you?' said an accusing voice.

'I'm fine, thanks,' I said, rather too jauntily. 'I'm here to see Vera. Only she's asleep, so . . . I thought I'd wait. If that's OK.'

'Are you a relative?' the woman asked, and it was clear she didn't like the cut of my jib.

'No, a friend. Of the family. I have been here before. Has she . . . is she likely to be asleep for long?'

It was a stupid question and she evidently thought so too.

'I don't know, dear. It's hard to say.'

'Yes. Quite. But she's . . . OK?'

'She has her good days and her bad days,' she said over her shoulder as she headed towards the kitchen. 'Do you want a cup of tea?'

'Oh, actually, that would be . . .' but she'd already gone. I was still holding the chair, so I took it over to Vera and quietly placed it in her eyeline, ready for when she woke up. Then I worried that it might be too much of a shock if the first thing she saw was an unfamiliar person right in front of her. So I moved it slightly to her right. But that put me uncomfortably close to the chair of the woman next to her, so I shuffled myself further left instead. That felt better. Or perhaps too far away. I shuffled back in a smidgen. There. That was it. As close to perfection as I could get it – given the imperfect situation.

I watched her sleeping for a moment or two and tried to get a sense of what mood she might be in. She looked peaceful enough, but then she would, wouldn't she? I wondered if, on waking, she'd be instantly overcome by the despair she felt last time. The 'where am I, who am I and *why* am I?' incomprehension had seemed too much for her to bear, and was certainly too awful for me to listen to.

I had no way of knowing how much of her days and nights were spent like that. If last time she was depressed, then the time before, she'd been belligerent and aggressive, as if my being here – whoever the hell I was – was an affront to her; as if I'd come to watch her misery for entertainment. And it had made me question visiting her even more. Since she didn't remember who I was, was there some part of her consciousness wondering what this stranger was doing, peering at her confusion? Maybe this wasn't just a pointless exercise; maybe I was making things worse.

I looked away, because now that I thought about it, it was kind of creepy, watching someone sleep. I glanced around the room, with an all-purpose, non-threatening smile on my face. Most of the other residents (patients? guests? I wondered what the acceptable terminology might be) were watching TV or staring into the middle distance. But one, a man I'd seen before, was watching me.

He was younger than the rest, and in the context of so many shrunken old people he seemed preternaturally big. His arms and legs were splayed around the sides of the chair as if he were a giant in a schoolroom. I smiled at him and he called something out to me – a loud bark of a monosyllable.

'Sorry?' I said. 'I didn't quite . . .'

He made the sound again, only this time it was part of a sentence. A question, I thought, judging by the tilt of his head. I got up and walked a little closer.

'I'm so sorry,' I said again. 'I didn't hear you.'

I knew that whatever sound he made next I would have to pretend to understand – there are only so many times you can feign not hearing before you have to have a stab at answering.

He spoke again. No. Still no clue. I felt awful about it – like I'd failed to make the effort. Presumably somebody here would know what he wanted, but there were no staff members in the room. And he didn't have an air of urgency about him. I took a punt that it wasn't life or death and went for bland sociability in return.

'Yeah . . .' I said, with my non-threatening smile. 'I know.'

He was still looking at me, and I sensed he expected more.

'I'm here to see Vera,' I began, and gestured towards her for clarification.

He barked something in reply, which I failed to understand again, but he too nodded towards the sleeping Vera, so he'd understood me at least.

'She's asleep,' I said, redundantly. And then, because he was looking at me so expectantly 'How are you today?'

He answered me with a half-smile and some words I couldn't fathom. I wondered if it would be rude to go back to my seat now. Instead I shifted from foot to foot a moment longer, so he wouldn't think I was tired of being with him. After a moment, he stopped looking at me and glanced up at the TV screen.

'Well . . . I'll leave you to it,' I said gauchely, as if I'd wandered uninvited into somebody's office and suddenly realised they had work to do. I went back to the chair in front of Vera's and pretended to look for something important in my bag. I wasn't sure how long I could keep this up. Perhaps I could just go. After all, she didn't know I was there and she probably wouldn't even when she saw me. The carers might think it was odd that I'd left after only – God, was it really only five minutes? But surely that wasn't what these visits were about . . . impressing the carers with what a good girl I was. Or was it? I mean, if not that then what *was* the point? If Vera didn't know me, then all I was doing was making myself feel virtuous, sacrificing my morning to be with someone who'd rather I hadn't bothered. Maybe I should go.

I reached down to get my bag and as I was standing up with it, I noticed Vera stir slightly. For an awful moment, I had the urge to run. Now, before she woke up, before the clock started on a visit that – propriety demanded – had to be at least twenty minutes. There was nobody to tell on me, no one would notice, except possibly the young giant, and the chances were if he said anything they wouldn't understand him. God, that was a terrible thing to think. What was wrong with me? But then again, running away wasn't a crime. It was weak, yes. Possibly borderline immoral, avoiding a situation simply because it was so damned miserable. But no jury in the land would convict me. It's what we'd all want to do in the circumstances.

The panic passed and I sat back down again. I knew I had to stay. I couldn't have told you why at that moment and I'm not sure I could even now, but walking away would have been wrong. It was a plain, old-fashioned sense of duty, I suppose. Sometimes you have to do things you don't want to do. God knows, Vera had spent a lifetime doing things *she* hadn't wanted to do. I felt I owed her this much, so I put my bag back on the floor and waited for her to slowly focus her eyes.

'Hello, Vera,' I said at last. She frowned at me and turned her head away.

'It's me. Rebecca. Do you remember me?'

There was a long pause while she pointedly stared at anything other than me. Then finally she turned her head back and said in a tone of infinite weariness, 'What do you want?'

'I wanted to come and see you,' I lied. 'Find out how you were doing.'

She turned her head away and again I felt overwhelmed by the futility of this whole enterprise.

'Go away,' she said in the same exhausted voice.

'OK. I will in a minute,' I replied. I looked at the floor, and she looked as far away from me as the stiffness in her neck would allow.

After a minute's pause, I said, 'Your tea's gone cold, Vera. Do you want me to ask for another one?'

She didn't immediately answer, but finally her eyes flickered down to the joyless-looking cup on her side table, and she seemed to recall, perhaps many years ago, someone having mentioned it.

'I want a cup of tea,' she said.

'I'll get you one.' I was only too glad to have something to do, some purpose to fulfil. I stood up and looked around for a member of staff. I could hear voices in the kitchen area, so I wandered over to it, doing a particular walk I remembered seeing my mother do in situations like this: tense shoulders, arms bent up at the elbows, fists clenched. It was meant to convey, 'I'm new here, I'm trying not to get in your way, I don't want to interrupt anything, I know you've got a lot to be getting on with.' But I suspect it just looked weird. There were two care assistants standing in the kitchenette, sharing a joke about something or other – possibly my ridiculous walk. One of them – the woman who'd earlier thought I was stealing the chair – looked at me.

'Hi,' I began. 'Sorry to be a nuisance, but I wonder if I could get a cup of tea for Vera.'

'She's got a cup of tea, dear,' said the one who didn't trust me.

'I know, but she was asleep and now it's gone cold.'

'OK, I'll bring her one,' she said. And then, with almost imperceptibly narrowed eyes, added, 'Are you a relative?'

'No. A friend. Of the family. Or rather, she's a friend of my family. I don't know her family very well.' Why was I making such heavy weather of this?

'Is she expecting you?' the woman asked, and it struck me as an odd thing to say of a woman with dementia. Surely one of the defining characteristics was that she wasn't expecting anyone, or anything – that every second of every day was new and random and terrifying.

'I've been here before,' I explained, since I couldn't answer the question, 'only she doesn't remember, of course.'

The woman nodded and said she'd bring the tea over in a moment. I thanked her rather more profusely than was warranted, and made my way back to Vera.

'It's on its way,' I said.

She turned to look at me. The look became a stare, and a frowning, dismissive one at that.

'The cup of tea. You wanted some tea, so . . . it's on its way.'

The frown continued.

'You're looking well,' I said. 'They've cut your hair.'

Silence.

'It looks lovely.'

Silence.

'Your hair. They've done a nice job.'

Where was that tea?

'Bouncy.' What? 'It looks bouncy. Your hair. In a good way.'

I looked around, but there was no sign of the woman I'd spoken to.

'The lady said she'd bring you a cup of tea in a minute.'

Silence.

'Mum sends her love.'

How much longer?

'I don't know if you remember Mum. Or Dad. I'm Rebecca? Does that sound at all . . . ring any . . . bring back some . . .?'

By now, every fibre of my being was telling me this was wrong, misguided, selfish even. I was confusing an already confused woman with my inane wittering. There must be some better way than this to help her. Or maybe not. Maybe she was beyond any help. Maybe all that anyone could do was to provide food and medication and the odd cup of tea, and I couldn't even do that. I felt myself getting irrationally angry that no one had any power in this scenario – least of all Vera. I wanted to go back to the kitchenette and demand tea for Vera *now*, not in five minutes' time but now. Because, God knows, she didn't have anything else to look forward to.

All this anger and frustration and, yes, fear was coursing through me when I suddenly became aware that Vera had said something.

'Rose?'

'No. Rebecca. Do you remember? You're a friend of my parents. I used to come and see you in your flat.'

'I remember you.'

This was progress.

'Do you?' I said eagerly. 'We used to chat in your front room. About the old days. I brought you some Bourbon biscuits because you said they reminded you of –'

'You're Rose.'

OK. It wasn't going to be plain sailing, but at least she was communicating with me. Or with somebody.

'Not Rose, Vera. Rose was your cousin. I'm Rebecca. My mum and dad knew you a long time ago, and –'

'Where's Walter?'

Walter? Walter. The baby cousin. Rose's brother.

'I'm not Rose, Vera. I'm Rebecca. Easily confused because . . . they both begin with an "R". But Rose was your cousin. When you were a young girl, and –'

'Where's little Walter? He's always getting into mischief. Where is he?'

This was the longest, most coherent thing I'd heard Vera say for a very long time, but I didn't know how to respond, because if I was honest, then I'd have to say, 'Walter's dead. Almost certainly dead. You've outlasted most of your generation. So the people you think of as your friends, your relatives, your baby cousins, are all of them long gone now.' How could I possibly say that to her? And what would be the point? I'd be telling her something devastating which she would grieve about for a moment, then instantly forget and have to be told all over again. I couldn't do it, I wouldn't do it, and I was – for the first time that day – absolutely confident I *shouldn't* do it.

I was framing my mouth for another attempt to remind her about my parents and the Bourbon biscuits when a thought occurred to me. What if I said I *was* Rose? I remembered all the stories I'd been told about the family and the house and the school they'd walked to together every day. And I'm an actor; I can improvise. Accept and build, those are the basic rules: never say no to the other person's suggestions, just acknowledge them and take them forward. I may not have been able to secure her a cup of tea, but here was something I might not be totally bloody useless at. It was certainly worth a go.

'I haven't seen Walter,' I began truthfully. 'Where do you think he might be?'

She sat silently for a minute and I wondered if the question had plunged her deeper into confusion. But then a faint smile crept over her face and she murmured: 'Hiding.'

'I bet you're right,' I said, feeling a buzz of excitement, as though a door long closed had opened.

'Are you Rose?' she asked again.

Accept and build, I thought, and answered with a little trepidation, 'Yes. Do you remember me?'

The smile was broader now. Her whole body suddenly seemed to relax.

'We lived in Twickenham,' she said softly. It was in the past tense, I noticed. She didn't think she was there now. She knew it was a memory, but it was one she could reach, something comprehensible and pleasant in an otherwise scary world.

'In the two-up, two-down,' I said, deliberately using one of Vera's own phrases. 'With Auntie Alice and Uncle Bert. And all the cousins . . .'

'Little Walter,' said Vera, and she chuckled. She actually laughed. It was a thing I never imagined I'd see her do again.

'Yes,' I said. 'He was always getting into mischief, wasn't he?'

She laughed again, and looked at me searchingly.

'Rose?'

'Yes.'

'I remember you,' she said.

I reached forward and took her hand.

'Well, I remember you too,' I said. 'Good to see you again, Vera.'

THE RELUCTANT VOLUNTEER

From the moment you have a child, you become, by definition, ill-equipped. Prior to that, you've probably had no experience of looking after anyone but yourself (or maybe, if you're a nicer person than me, your partner). Now suddenly here you are, left alone for twenty-four hours a day with this most vulnerable of creatures, aware that everything you do and don't do is of life or death importance.

Over those first few months and years, as you grow in experience and your child in independence, you might think this feeling of inadequacy would pass. But it doesn't. It gets worse. And the main thing that keeps you in a permanent state of Not Being Good Enough is the school parents' association.

Once your kids get to senior school, the Parents' and Teachers' Association, or whatever they call themselves, will be the preserve of die-hard fundraisers: the willing, the eager, the selfless, the doers and the joiners. But at primary school, you're all expected to get stuck in. There's no point telling them you're too busy because, hell, we're *all* busy.

It's just that some of us are willing to go the extra mile for our children.

In fact, the whole PTA edifice is founded on a solid bedrock of guilt from those early years of parenting, during which – no matter how hard you've tried – you know that somehow or other you've screwed things up.

Thus, the call for 'volunteers' carries with it a faint hope of redemption: help out at the school fete and you might undo some of the damage you've done to your child. And what about contributing something to those children less fortunate than your own? Their blighted lives are almost certainly your fault too, somehow or other. Really, an afternoon here or there . . . would it kill you?

Don't imagine the call won't come, because there's no escape. You have to be in that playground every day at three thirty. You can try not to catch a committee member's eye, you can check your phone, hide behind the climbing frame or feign myopia, but they will find you.

Now as it happens, I don't consider myself to be a bad parent. My kids have one or two issues with me, it's true, one of these being the way I wake them up in the mornings. Not being a natural early bird myself, I always try on school days to inject a little cheer. But it turns out a daily rendition of 'Good Morning' from *Singin' in the Rain* isn't the way to go. It's a shame, because I've almost nailed the choreography, but hey, once I've been told a thing is irritating fifty or sixty times I can take a hint. Show-tunes aside, though, I think I'm a decent kind of mother, and until one of them writes their own version of *Mommie Dearest*, you'll have to take my word for it.

Does that qualify me to be useful to the Parents' Associ-ation? No, the mere fact that I've procreated does that. I'm in whether I like it or not.

I'm not afraid of hard work, but I baulk at having to work hard and still do a thing badly. I write and I act – that's my skill set. I don't make things or organise or corral support. I can't sell, I'm too shy to leaflet and I don't like talking to strangers.

These weaknesses are surmountable of course. Not so my greater failings, like my poor mental arithmetic and total lack of common sense. The latter means I don't think ahead and plan around what could go wrong. The former, that I panic when customers want more than one item or the correct change. And another thing: tombolas, raffles, silent auctions, all that sort of thing – I genuinely don't understand them. Which ones do you buy tickets for in ad-vance, and which ones do you get prizes for there and then, and how do you know how much you should bid? It's just one of those gaps in my education; perhaps I was off school when they explained it all.

Baking? Also not my forte. And even if it was, I wouldn't let on. Every bloody week, there's another cake sale; it's a full-time job. My friend Fran once rang me the night before her kids' summer fete in a panic. Three weeks earlier, in a moment of weakness, she'd promised to supply ten cakes for the cake stall. Ten. All different. When she signed up, she thought she had plenty of time. She could pace herself: three a week and a tray of brownies at the last minute was a challenge, but she was pretty sure she could meet it. It was the night after she'd made the offer that she woke up in a cold sweat, having suddenly realised that you can't make cakes three weeks in advance. Fruit cakes, maybe – they'll keep for years; you can eat a slice of wedding cake on your twenty-fifth anniversary and it'll still taste as burnt, dry and joyless as if it were baked yesterday. But at a summer fete, people want treats: light, airy sponges, indulgent chocolate tortes – the sort of things we don't have time to make for ourselves. This was what Fran was expected to deliver. Not wanting to let people down, she'd spent those three weeks stockpiling flour and sugar like a sweet-toothed survivalist. That morning, she'd embarked on an increasingly foul-tempered marathon of a baking session, and now at 9 p.m. she was begging me through tears of exhaustion to search my cupboards for edible sprinkles.

But if you don't sign up for something, if you think you can just pay your 50p entrance fee and wander round looking at stuff, then you've got another think coming. Phil never volunteered for anything, being very much of the opinion that if he gave the PTA a thirty-quid donation, he could stay home watching football on the day of the fete and they'd still be up on the deal. So it was no small surprise when one year, towards the end of the proceedings, I heard his voice through a loud hailer. He'd arrived at four o'clock, when he thought things would be winding down, and got collared to run the auction. It turned out he was rather good at it, and in a mere fifteen minutes' showing-off with a megaphone, he made £500 more than I had in four hours of 'guess the name of the teddy'.

Anyway, after the first few years of misery, when I got roped into being a 'floater' – going from stall to stall whenever someone needed a break and never knowing what I was doing on any of them, I finally realised that I'd better take some control. When your options are limited, you have to get in early. I monitored the newsletters so that I could be at the very first meeting and pounced on the activity I thought I could handle.

I signed up for the 'creative' tables. There were three: Sand Art, Bead Making and Glass Painting. They sounded simple, uncontentious and pleasantly dull, and the other volunteers and I decided we would circulate between the three to avoid going completely mad with boredom.

On the day of the fete, I got there early to set up. There was a lot to do, of course, but nothing that couldn't be done in half an hour or so. It seemed to me the real point of being there early was being seen to be busy. There was much frowning and nodding, rolling-up of sleeves and mopping of brows, and a good deal of ostentatious initiative-showing.

'I'll get some tea organised.'

'I've brought my own tarpaulin.'

'I've got a gazebo.'

'I've got £200 worth of fifty-pence pieces.'

And on and on. Everyone wanted a nod of approval, a pat on the back, a cry of 'What would we do without you?' If you could get yourself a mention in the following week's newsletter ('Special thanks to x without whose y none of this would have been possible'), then your place in PTA Heaven was assured.

Once we were all up and running, my first stop was Sand Art. On the table were eight trays of coloured sand: red, yellow, blue, green, pink, white, purple and glittery black. I was given a box full of novelty-shaped plastic bottles and a set of scoops. The idea was that your customer paid their money, chose a bottle and filled it with whatever array of colours took their fancy. It really couldn't be simpler. The money side should have been easy too, since every turn cost the same, regardless of the type of bottle. But this, it quickly became apparent, was where the scheme fell down. My first few takers were put out to discover that the four-scoop wiggly worm bottle cost the same as the six-scoop elephant. I could see their point, but was reluctant to have the stress of differential pricing. In the face of growing dissent, however, I caved in and took a quiet moment to write down a crib sheet for myself telling me how much change I should give a child with a £5 note, say, wanting a 75p camel.

As it turned out, mental arithmetic was the least of my problems. Three kids in succession handed over £10 notes and I quickly ran out of change altogether. I couldn't see the woman with the float, so rather than turn customers away I substituted some of my own money. But then I remembered I was supposed to be keeping a detailed tally of income and bottles sold, since the unsold bottles would be returned to the suppliers. The money I'd put in as change wouldn't match my sales, and worried that this goodwill gesture might inexplicably start to look like fraud, I began to get hopelessly confused. I only had one child filling a bottle at this point, so I sat down with my crib sheet again to work it all out, but when I looked up, I noticed he had used the wrong scoops for the wrong colours. The pristine trays of sand were now polluted. I waited for him to finish, then started vainly trying to pick individual grains of yellow sand out of the purple box. It was hopeless, of course, and made even more futile when a sudden gust of wind sent large quantities of every colour gaily flying across the school field. Some of it got into one child's eye, so I had to run and get him a wet tissue. When I came back, he and his friend had tipped the entire blue tray into the white tray and sprinkled in a bit of green for devilment.

When the time came to change stalls, I handed over to my successor eight trays of muddy-coloured sand and a random amount of money. It was threatening to rain, and I figured she wouldn't question my bookkeeping once the sand started turning into cement.

I went indoors to take over Bead Art. This, as the name suggested, gave children a chance to make their own jewellery. There was a selection of beads of all colours and sizes, and two lengths of thread – bracelets were 50p, necklaces £1. My first customer was a little girl from my daughter's class. She paid her pound, and sat down opposite me to begin threading. She was adorably polite – every time she took a bead, she thanked me as though they were my personal property. And she was also impressively diligent, taking enormous pains to choose which bead would look best with which, and to grade them according to size, so that the biggest would lie at the front of her neck and the smallest near the nape. When at last she handed me her completed work, I told her how proud she should be of it, tied the two ends together and handed it back to her. But as she took it, I watched in a kind of slow-motion horror as the knot I'd tied unravelled and every single bead clattered to the floor. I gave her another go free, of course, partly because I felt so guilty, and partly because her sobbing was bad for business. When she'd finished necklace two, I carefully tied it around her neck with a double knot, to prevent it happening again and she skipped away very happily. I saw her mother the next day; apparently I'd tied it so thoroughly, they'd had to cut it off her. Realising she could never wear it again broke her heart for a second time.

Glass Painting was the third of the craft activities. This, surely, must be idiot-proof. All I had to do was give the customer a coloured glass pebble and let them decorate it with the special ink pens. Most of them opted for writing their names (kids have an egotistical need to stamp their identity on inanimate objects), and although the pens were rather blobby, it all worked pretty well. I then explained to them, as detailed in my instruction leaflet, that the ink must be allowed to dry, and asked them to come back after half an hour. But the ink wasn't dry after half an hour; not even after an hour and a half. The kids got tired of waiting, and even though I offered a refund they wanted to take their pebbles home. So I let them, with a stern warning that the designs would smear and stain their clothes.

When I saw a committee member heading my way, I naturally assumed there'd been a complaint. If I'm honest, I was praying I'd be asked to leave.

'Could you do me a favour,' she said, 'and take over from Liz on Hook-a-Duck? She needs . . . a break.'

I should have noticed the pause, but I didn't. Not until it was too late.

'Sure,' I said, 'but you might want to think about closing Glass Painting down. We can't afford the cleaning bills.'

The Hook-a-Duck stall was hard to miss – a paddling pool filled with bright yellow plastic ducks with hooks on their heads. It had quite a throng of people round it, and there in the centre, perched on a camping stool and looking harassed, was Liz.

'Oh thank God,' she said when she spotted me. She whipped off her money belt and thrust it at me.

'Fifty pence a go, a lucky-dip prize if they catch one, the hooks are there.'

As she got up to go, she squeezed my arm.

'Good luck,' she said, without a hint of a smile.

'Will I need it?' I laughed.

'Yes,' she said, mirthlessly. 'Yes, you will.'

For some reason, Hook-a-Duck seemed to bring out the absolute worst in human behaviour. Otherwise civilised people, good citizens of unblemished character, got within an ace of it and became rabid dogs. There was pushing and shoving, snatching of hooks, jumping of queues, accusations of cheating ... it was as if the world were ending and the only survivors would be those who'd managed to skewer a rubber duck on the end of a pole. One set of people was thrusting money at me and demanding change while another set was clutching hooks to their chests so no one else could get them. I tried appealing for calm, getting them to form an orderly line, but my pleading voice was drowned in the chaos. Eventually I lost it – I'm only human, after all, and it had been a trying sort of a day.

'Right, everybody stop talking!' I yelled at the top of my voice.

There are times when drama school vocal training comes in handy.

'No one's having any turns until you give me the hooks.'

There was a pause in hostilities and an embarrassed shuffling of feet. I collected up the hooks.

'Now form a queue, please.'

'My son was here before your daughter . . . ' said one aggrieved parent to another. I shot them the kind of look my mother used when teaching seven-year-olds. It seemed to work. Order was restored; a line appeared. I addressed the person at the head of it.

'Have you paid for your turn?' I asked.

'Yes,' he said, meekly. I ceremoniously handed over a hook.

'You have two minutes to hook a duck. Time begins . . . now.'

It was the one thing I'd succeeded at all day. And why? Because it didn't involve money or knowledge or sales technique. It involved parenting skills. And being a parent was something I could do. I had experience. It was also, ironically, what had got me into this mess in the first place.

When I got home at the end of the fete, I was exhausted. My feet ached, I had multi-coloured sand in every facial orifice and my clothing was smeared with never-drying ink.

'How much did you make this year?' Phil asked, handing me a large drink. 'Was it worth it?'

'Oh yes,' I said with great confidence. 'I did four different stalls, so it was knackering, but *my* takings alone came to about . . .'

I starting totting it up.

'All in all . . .'

I hoped it was my maths letting me down again, otherwise this was too depressing.

'. . . including the £10 change I put in at the beginning . . . about £33.50.'

He was right. We should have just sent a cheque.

A few months later, the juggernaut was starting up again. This time it was for the Christmas Fayre, an event that had to be bigger and better and more festive than the summer one, if only to justify its faux-archaic spelling. My heart sank at the prospect of going through it all again.

As it happened, the carol concert was planned for the same week as the Fayre, and Emma, who was organising the music, stopped me one day at home time.

'I like to do a set piece in the middle of the carols every year. And this year, because the children have been learning the song from *The Snowman*, I thought maybe you could tell the story.'

As long as I did *something* for the school coffers at Christmas, I'd be in the clear. And Emma's idea, being effectively an acting gig where I didn't have to learn any lines, sounded right up my alley. All I had to do was rehearse it with her a couple of times, so that I knew when to start speaking and when to shut up, and let the music work its magic. I said yes, and when the PTA came asking, I told them with great relief that I was spoken for.

The idea was that I would tell an abbreviated version of the story, and at the climax of the piece, when Emma began to play the famous 'Walking in the Air' song, all the children in the audience – being by then familiar with it – would join in and sing it for their parents.

My son and daughter were aged around ten and eight at this point – old enough to feel self-conscious at the thought of their mother making a spectacle of herself. As soon as I told them about this *Snowman* thing, they were dead set against it. They got it into their heads that I was going to sing the song on my own in front of the entire audience, and I firmly reassured them that was not going to happen. Mine was a speaking-only part, not least because 'Walking in the Air' was written for a boy soprano, not a middle-aged mother of two. So, reluctantly, they agreed to be there.

The concert began and people gradually lost their inhibitions and sang along to 'O Come, All Ye Faithful' and 'God Rest Ye Merry Gentlemen'. It was all mulled-wine-and-mince-pie marvellous.

Halfway through, Emma did her introduction and I stood up to read the *Snowman* story.

School halls aren't known for their great acoustics. In Emma's living room, it hadn't been a problem making myself heard over the piano, but here with a high ceiling and a lot of hard surfaces, I really needed a microphone. There wasn't one, so there was nothing for it but to use that theatrical voice I'd last deployed as a weapon to quell the Hook-a-Duck rebellion. Having moments before been chatting to people casually, I now had to speak from the diaphragm and over-enunciate. The effect was a combination of Peggy Mount and Julie Andrews. In the front row, my kids sat mortified. Why was I standing in their school hall shouting poshly at all their friends?

I could sense their unease, but like all performers, I believed that I could overcome it with confidence. Experience had taught me that if you feel uncertain, the audience will feel uncertain. 'If in doubt, go for it' was my motto. So I savoured each word and sold each syllable, but I couldn't help glancing at them from time to time and seeing their eyes burning into me like little lasers of hatred.

Emma had, as she'd promised, explained at the outset that the children were expected to join in with 'Walking in the Air', so as I finished the story, and she played the opening chords, I gave a very clear gesture to the audience that this was their moment. But nobody joined in. They all just sat there looking at me. OK, I thought, maybe they need someone to start them off. I warbled the opening phrase. Still the audience stared at me. And with Emma still hammering it out on the piano, there was nothing for it but to carry on. In case you don't know, the song 'Walking in the Air' is at least an octave too high for me. Imagine the opening solo from the Nine Lessons and Carols being hijacked by a female pub singer, and you'll have a sense of what it must have sounded like. I tried to maintain my earlier confidence, but inwardly I was dying and outwardly I was taking everyone else with me.

When it ended, there was a smattering of polite applause and I went to sit down next to my kids. For some time, they stared ahead of them in rigid embarrassment. Finally, Ollie turned to me, glowered, and whispered:

'Why did you *do* that?'

'I was trying to help,' I whispered back.

'Well don't. Don't ever try to help again,' he pleaded.

I smiled at him and shook my head.

'If only it were that easy,' I said.

PUTTING AWAY CHILDISH THINGS

'Wanna play a game?'

The tinny, computerised voice came from the bottom of a bin bag. At Tilly's request, I was throwing away some of the toys she no longer played with. She was twelve now, and needed the space for clothes and hair straighteners. One or two things were allowed to remain, mainly the cutest of her cuddly animals, but anything too childish was to be taken to a charity shop or chucked.

The voice was emanating from a little, palm-sized, electronic playhouse. Inside it was the rudimentary animated figure of a girl. She looked like a 1960s teenager: bobby socks, flicky hair and a skirt that stuck out like a triangle. The way the toy worked was that you moved this cartoon girl around her mini-home, and she would 'interact' with you through a series of repeated statements. As I'd tried to dispose of it, I must have inadvertently pressed one of its buttons, and brought her to life. I could see the playhouse lit up through the black skin of the bin bag, and as I rummaged to get it out, the girl gave a jaunty whistle signifying her impatience.

'What's taking you so long?' the voice said, and I remembered why Tilly had tired of it. It was a toy that made demands on your time. It wasn't content to sit there and wait. Once you'd made the mistake of waking it up, it would go on nagging you and nagging you until you felt like hurling it across the room.

I pulled it from underneath the other bits of rubbish, and wondered why I hadn't put it in the charity-shop pile.

'Come *on*,' said the voice, imploringly. 'Let's play. It's a beautiful day. We're gonna have some fun.'

That was why. There was no 'off' switch. There were buttons for every other function: you could change the girl's clothes, and give her some food; you could get her to dance and make her laugh. But you couldn't shut her up. You had to wait until the damn thing went into 'sleep' mode. It was a war of attrition; a siege. The only way to win was to wait. I suppose I hadn't wanted to inflict it on anyone else.

I sat back on my heels and looked at it for a while. The pixelated minx stood with her hands on her hips and looked right back at me.

'Wanna dance?' she asked. I carried on looking.

'Wanna hear a joke?'

I waited a little longer, but the playhouse was still lit up, which meant the girl was awake, and it felt somehow rude to ignore her.

'Wanna go to the park?' she asked. 'Wanna bake cookies?'

'Wanna belt up?' I countered. There was a long silence. Then the jaunty whistle again.

'I know a game,' piped the voice.

'Please, I'm begging you, shut up now!' I shouted. Another silence. Maybe it was winding down. And then:

'Come on, lazybones,' she said in a Shirley Temple voice, simultaneously cute and imperious, and I decided enough was enough.

I carried the toy down to the kitchen and tried to find a screwdriver. The only way to turn it off was to take out its batteries. But none of the screwdrivers was the right size, and while my search got increasingly frantic she carried on whistling, sighing and giving theatrical yawns.

'Let's have lunch.' 'Wanna go to the park?' 'Let's go swimming.' 'Come on, lazybones!'

I found the right screwdriver, and just as she was offering yet again to show me her bloody dance, I removed the back of the toy, took out its batteries, ran upstairs with it and triumphantly shoved it in the rubbish.

When Ollie was a toddler he called cucumber 'mu-nu'. It was one of his favourite things to eat. One day Phil threw some cucumber out of the fridge because it had gone off, and when I asked him why he'd done it, Ollie copied his father's grimace and said, by way of explanation, 'Daddy mu-nu urgh.' It was his first sentence.

Tilly, at the age of two or three, was given to declamatory statements, as if her life were accompanied by a fanfare. 'The biggest blueberry in the world has just been tooken and etten,' she'd announce as she stuffed it into her mouth.

Both of these memories are clear to me because, for a while, I had a notebook and wrote things down. Sometimes it would be an anecdote, sometimes a mispronunciation. They were incidental things which I knew I'd forget if I didn't make a note of them. As the kids got older, they'd sometimes ask to see the book. It made them laugh and I think it stirred in them some vague recollection of being tiny and safe and puzzled by the world.

When both children were in infants' school, I bought Phil a video camera, but he never used it. I was cross at first, until he explained to me that he wanted to be a part of their childhood, and not just view it through a lens. And as the years passed, we went to their school plays and assemblies and sports days and parties, and saw parents endlessly, obsessively filming, and I started to think that he was right. Once you've recorded one child's walk-on part in the end-of-term show, you have to film the other child's guitar recital, and on and on, because it's impossible to say, 'This time, I'm going to just sit and watch.' For us, it was important to be present rather than to keep a record. We took photos, of course, and with the advent of mobile phones, that got easier to do. We could capture a moment instantly, without having the forethought to bring a camera or buy film. But we had virtually no moving footage of their squeaky voices and uninhibited games, and it was only once they'd both left primary school, once Ollie's voice got deeper and Tillie swapped playfulness for poise, that I came to regret our decision.

It was my parents' ability to accumulate stuff that turned me into a thrower. When I got my own place, I decided I would regularly clear out books and shoes and unwanted detritus. We encouraged the children to do the same. We got rid of clothes as they outgrew them, and picture books to make way for ones with chapters. We only kept things that we really 'needed' to keep. But that concept of 'need' is an ever-changing one, and entirely individual. It has nothing to do with actual need – the stuff you have to have in order to survive. It's about the things you want, and the things you feel you ought to have, because all your friends have them. But it's also about the things that, like the entries in my notebook, make you feel safe and secure. As we get older, and realise, in theory at least, that cuddly toys aren't going to protect you from monsters, we talk about them having 'sentimental value' instead, but that's just another way of saying we still need them. Of course anything, if you hold on to it long enough, will acquire sentimental value, but you can't keep everything. Well not in my house, you can't. So the trick is second-guessing what will retain its status in the 'need' pile, and what has become redundant. That's why when Tilly had airily suggested giving away her Barbie dolls, I'd sneakily hidden them in a drawer. I remember outgrowing mine at that age, but I also know the pleasure I got from digging them out again when she first got hers. In the end, it came down to the quality of memories attached to a particular book or toy. If you'd had endless fun with a thing, or felt a warm glow every time you looked at a particular illustration in a book, then it was probably best to keep it. If you felt nothing very much, you could pass it on to the charity shop where it had a chance of being better appreciated by someone else.

We got rid of bags and bags of stuff, and most of the time it felt liberating. But occasionally, we'd experience the bitter pang of regret that we'd made a mistake and we'd never see that thing again. And often that regret didn't come from the kids, but from Phil and me.

Because the fact that they no longer 'needed' stuff wasn't all good news. Of course it was great that they were growing up, moving forward, expanding their horizons and all of that. But that meant that alongside the teddies and the magic sets, they were leaving behind the 'mu-nus' and the 'tookens'. And once they'd figured out that a cuddly cat couldn't keep the monsters at bay, it was only a matter of time before they realised that we couldn't either. And soon, too soon, we too would have merely sentimental value, rather than actually being needed.

After the demise of the animated playhouse, I carried on sorting through Tilly's toys. The charity-shop pile was tee-tering now under the weight of her old stuff: her hobby horse, her My Little Ponies, her jigsaws. The rubbish and recycling bags were groaning too: stacks of old comics, playing cards with sweets stuck to them, sticker books, dried-out felt-tips.

I stopped for a minute and looked at what was there. Some of it, much of it, meant nothing; things she'd been given as presents by friends who didn't know her taste; toys she'd hardly looked at. But stuck to many of the items, as firmly as the sweet to the playing card, was a memory of her sitting on that floor – sometimes with me, sometimes with Phil or Ollie or a school friend – deeply, profoundly absorbed in some game. There were the plastic beads that we'd strung together into hideous, garish bracelets, and the toy car that had taken Barbie to her wedding – an elaborate affair, which had occupied an entire Saturday afternoon.

She'd asked me to get rid of this stuff because she knew she was never going to play with it again, and all of a sudden that thought gripped my heart. She was never going to play with it again, which meant, I supposed, that she was never going to play with me again – not really, not in the same way. I could still be a part of her new interests, of course. We could watch stupid videos together and talk about clothes. We could paint our nails and sing together. I was still needed, but not in the way I used to be.

For one insane moment, I thought about putting the batteries back in the electronic playhouse. Yes, it was irritating, but more than anything I wanted to sit on the floor of that room, and hear again a small, imperious voice saying, 'Come on, lazybones. Let's bake cookies. Wanna play a game?'

MORE BY ACCIDENT THAN DESIGN

If I squint and peer as far back into my career as possible, I can just about remember a time when people had regular meetings over lunch. I can even remember there being a proper sit-down restaurant at the BBC, where a waiter brought you food on a china plate and placed it on a white tablecloth. I only ate there once, during a break in rehearsals with an old-school comic, and we even drank wine without anyone arching an eyebrow and writing us off as unemployable lushes. But shortly afterwards the restaurant became a self-service canteen, and shortly after that a kiosk for pre-packed sandwiches.

The media, like almost every other industry, became a place that disapproved of a hearty lunch. Now we're all supposed to get by with a quick power snack while we dash off an email or ten. Taking a full hour is old school, and nobody, but nobody, drinks anything stronger than green tea.

So on the rare occasion that I get invited to a proper lunch meeting in a proper restaurant, I approach it with giddy anticipation.

A producer I'd wanted to meet for quite some time got in touch via my agent and suggested we discuss some ideas. I was delighted as he had a reputation as a guy who could make things happen. But I was even more pleased when he suggested the venue – a brand-new, chic-looking restaurant off Soho Square. It was the kind of place that was so cool it didn't even have its name outside. You were expected just to know it was there – if you had to ask, then it really wasn't the place for you.

Consequently, it took me a while to find it, having first tried to enter via a fire escape and then overshot the main door and stumbled into a dry cleaner's. But once I found my way inside, I could see from the minimal, monochrome reception area that I was in for a special experience. It turned out I was the first to arrive, so I left my coat and um-brella with the stunningly beautiful cloakroom attendant. Then a stunningly beautiful maître d' took me to the bar where a stunningly beautiful barman offered me a drink. Ordering alcohol is always high risk at a meeting. It can make you look either very nervous or like you couldn't give a shit. Plus there's always the chance that the other person is in rehab and you'll be rubbing their noses in their own abstinence. So I ordered water, but I asked for sparkling be-cause I wanted to look like I had about me a certain *je ne sais quoi*.

'Take a seat,' said the barman, and he gestured towards the central area of the bar. But there didn't appear to be any seats. There was instead an art installation consisting of five metallic stalks. Each stalk was about the height of a seven-year-old child, and had two discs, one where the child's knees would have been, the other in lieu of its shoulders.

That was it. Spikes and discs. I wandered up to them, trying to look casual. It was like a futuristic Stonehenge, a metal circle which clearly had some meaning and purpose, just not one that was instantly fathomable.

From behind me, I heard the barman calling out, 'Go ahead, take a seat. I'll bring your drink over to you,' so I figured that, in defiance of logic, this must be the place. I looked around to make sure he wasn't watching, and then stood close enough to one of the stalks to measure it up against me. The higher disc was way above the level of my hips, and significantly too small for even the pertest backside. But I wondered if I was meant to use the lower one for leverage, to propel me up to this inadequate perch. I checked again that nobody was there, then put my foot on the lower disc. It seemed stable enough, so I ventured transferring my weight on to it. But when I did, the whole stem wobbled precariously. I steadied myself by gripping on to a neighbouring stalk and managed to lift one buttock on to the upper disc. As I did so, I could hear the barman approaching with my drink. I'd committed myself now; there was no going back, so I rested there unsteadily, like a novice unicyclist. The barman handed me the glass without comment. It seemed I'd done the right thing and I felt un-accountably pleased with myself. I'd identified a chair and managed to sit on it. This was going to be a good day after all.

I took a few sips of water, dribbling much of it down my shirt as I kept losing my balance. And after a few moments, the producer arrived and apologised for keeping me wait-ing. I succeeded in lowering myself without incident from my eyrie, though I landed with a bump and spilled the rest of my drink on my trousers. But he didn't seem to notice, and the stunningly beautiful maître d' ushered us over to our table.

I saw with relief that it actually looked like a table and was surrounded by things which most of the world, and not just a handful of design students, might consider to be chairs. I relaxed a little and began the process of trying to appear intelligent and employable. We seemed to be getting off on the right foot, and I was midway through what I felt was a brief ice-breaker of an anecdote when a stunningly beautiful waiter arrived and buggered up the punchline.

'Would you like me to talk you through the menu?' he asked.

We said that we were fine just looking. But apparently we were mistaken.

'Only there's a concept to it,' he explained with the air of one who wished he'd taken that job in telesales after all.

'A concept?' I repeated.

'Yeah,' he said, with an apologetic tilt of his head.

'Ooh, sounds intriguing,' said the producer. 'Go ahead then.'

The concept, as far as I could grasp it, was this: the dishes on the menu weren't meals as you or I might know them. Rather they were small taster plates designed to show you what such a combination of ingredients might be like were one to have it as an actual meal. Somehow – I didn't quite catch how – this was better than having a whole portion of one thing that you fancied and, you know, eating it until you felt full. I guess it was like dining homoeopathy – the less you ate of something, the greater its effect on you would be. I was pretty sure the result would be that you'd go away hungry. But no, the creators of the concept had thought of that. We were advised to order several of these mini-meals each, and he assured us this wouldn't mean getting a mish-mash of uncomplementary flavours in our mouths, since the sum of these parts would make for a nicely cohesive whole.

Oh, and there was one more rule we needed to under-stand: we had to share.

Now, I'm happy to share food with my children or my husband. There are even some very close friends with whom I'll comfortably double dip. But I don't want to share food with a man I've never met, especially when I'm trying to impress him. I want my own plate, thank you very much. That way, I don't have to worry that I'm eating too much of the cheesy thing, or he's taken the last mushroom. And we don't get bogged down – as we now inevitably did – in an endless discussion of what we could and couldn't eat: 'Well, I'm a vegetarian, but if you're lactose intolerant then I guess we could go for the spinach and pine-nut frittata, unless that'll set off your nut allergy, which it shouldn't as I'm pretty sure pine nuts are a legume, but if you don't like spinach then I guess we'd be better off with some lentils, unless one of us suffers from IBS . . .'

Call me uptight, but when I go for a working lunch, I don't want to be forced into discussing bowel conditions. But somebody, somewhere had seriously thought this was a good idea. 'Let's open a restaurant that breaks with con-vention,' they'd probably declared, 'that subverts bourgeois notions of taste and individuality. Let's democratise the eating process; food is not something to be owned. And if that makes people feel uncomfortable and embarrassed and even a little bit icky – well then, we'll have shaken up the old world order, and the revolution will have succeeded.'

I'm not blind to the ills of society; I can see there's room for improvement. I just wouldn't have picked fine dining as the first battleground. But perhaps this was a wilfully literal interpretation of the theory that revolutions start with the middle classes.

When the food eventually began to arrive – 'It will all come at different times,' we'd been told, which was great, because waiting around and watching someone else eat is one of the things I look for in a restaurant experience – it was predictably fussy. Tiny stacks of whimsy marooned on a china sea, crispy curlicues and gossamer fronds and smears of froth that looked like a shrew's ejaculate, all tee-tering and collapsing as we tried to serve ourselves.

'Is this the aubergine thing?' the producer whispered, not wanting to betray his ignorance.

'I'm not sure,' I replied. 'I think the pomegranate seeds went with the feta, but I can't remember. Does it taste like aubergine?'

'Couldn't say. It's all so tiny that there's not really enough of it to taste. Looks great, though.'

I agreed enthusiastically. It all looked great: the food, the seating, the menu. But none of it did what you wanted it to do. The seating didn't support you, the menu didn't tell you anything, the food didn't fill you up. And to top it all, the producer and I were now so baffled and ill at ease, we'd run out of conversation. We both needed a moment to regroup, so I decided to go to the loo.

As the entrance to the ladies' swung shut I was plunged into near-darkness. It took a few seconds for my eyes to adjust, and when they had, it didn't help much. The whole interior was glazed in deep maroon. Running the length of one wall was a trough, which I took to be a sink. The door was behind me and at the far end there was either another woman dressed like me also looking confused, or a mirror. So I figured, by a process of elimination, that the cubicles were opposite the trough. But it looked like a solid wall. I peered at it for a bit, and could eventually make out some floor-to-ceiling cracks in the wall where the doors were separated. But how to open one? I pushed lightly, but nothing happened. I started to move crablike along the wall, hands outstretched, like Marcel Marceau in an imaginary box, until eventually something gave and a door swung smoothly inwards. There was a loo, thank goodness. It wasn't immediately apparent how I would flush it, but I took a wild guess that this might happen automatically, by virtue of some faintly sinister peeping Tom of a beam, and I was right. Getting out was easy, since the light was so dim and my fear of getting stuck in the cubicle so great that I'd propped the door open with my bag. Now all I had to do was wash my hands.

I stood in front of the trough and tried to put myself inside the head of the designer. I had quite a clear image by now of this smug neo-Bauhaus smart-arse trying to make the little people look stupid. Where would such a fiendish genius put taps, soap and towels? It would have to be the last place any normal person would look for them. I waved my hands over the trough like a sorcerer, hoping to make contact with another hidden beam. But no water appeared. I tapped my feet along the ground in search of pedals or footpads, but still nothing. I pressed the walls, prodded the splashback, waved vigorously and with increasing desperation. Still no water. I now realised, with embarrassment, that I'd been gone from the table for some time. What would my producer think I was doing in here? With a weary sigh, I accepted defeat, reached into my bag for a packet of wet wipes and cleaned my hands with those.

As I walked back to the table, I thought at first that he'd left. Then I realised that all the remaining dishes we'd ordered had, contrary to our waiter's warning, arrived at the same time. Each one looked taller and more impressive than the last, as if someone with nothing better to do had built a model of Manhattan out of food. The producer hadn't left, he was simply lost behind them.

I sat down and smiled at him. He looked rather helpless. It was difficult to know what any of it was, let alone how to share it between us. He gallantly attempted to airlift something on to my plate, but it broke up in mid-air, leaving shrapnel on my cardigan.

We stared disconsolately at it all, then at each other.

'Shall I get the bill?' he sighed.

The bill, like the food, was steep and hard to digest. Because we had no idea what we'd ordered, we couldn't possibly contest it, and it suddenly occurred to me that maybe that was the real 'concept' behind the menu. The producer kindly paid and we both stepped out into the sunshine. We shook hands and said we'd meet again. But I knew we wouldn't. Neither of us would want to be reminded that chic dining had defeated us. We went our separate ways feeling old and uncool. If this was how the world was going to be from now on, we too would need to be redesigned.

'Don't you worry,' my taxi driver said for the third time since I'd got in the back of his cab. 'I'm gonna get you there. Plenty of time.'

'That's great,' I said. 'And you know exactly where I mean?'

'Sure, sure. Just relax.'

'OK. Thank you.'

I sat back and forced a smile, in case he happened to glance at me in his rear-view mirror. But I had an uneasy feeling about this. Really uneasy. The traffic looked terrible, and I didn't know the city well enough to judge if we were taking the best route. I could always try to follow it on my phone, but the last time I did that abroad, it cost me twice my annual phone bill. Why hadn't I brought a map? I sneaked a look at my watch, and sure enough, he spotted it in the mirror. I wished he'd concentrate on the road.

'You got nothing to worry about, lady,' he said.

'No, I'm fine. It's just . . .'

'I'm gonna get you there.'

'Yes, it's not that. It's just, I don't know if I've left enough time.'

'I'll get you to the university, don't you worry.'

Oh no. He'd said it again. I thought we'd sorted this out.

'It's Universal City. Not the university. Universal City.'

'I got you.'

'And it's not the theme park. Not the part where the tourists go on the little bus thing. It's the studio. Gate 5 of the studio.'

'Gate 5,' he said reassuringly. 'You told me. I'm gonna get you there. Gate 5. University.'

'Yeah,' I said, wearily. 'Well no. Universal City.'

'OK, I heard you,' he said again. 'Relax.'

For twenty years, people had said to me, 'You should go to LA. Take some meetings. You'd love it out there.' But somehow the time had never seemed right. I liked the work I was doing in the UK. And my children were small and I didn't want to take them out of school, still less to leave them behind. But now they were almost grown up, and even my British agent had said there was no harm in trying my hand to see if anything came up. A quirky nanny? A down-at-heel aristocrat? The slightly snobby neighbour who turns out to have a heart of gold? They always want British actors for those kinds of parts, and it seemed crazy not even taking the first step. A meeting or two. Where would be the harm in that? So I got myself an American agent.

Carl was a powerhouse, an energetic pug-dog puppy of a man. He would call me up, and even without the LA phone code appearing on my display, I'd know it was him because he never said hello. He'd just launch straight in, as if the conversation we'd last had three weeks ago had never ended.

'So is it raining there? I know it's raining.'

'Oh hi, Carl. How are you doing?'

'Hot. That's how I'm doing. Not even hot. Pleasantly warm. It's a balmy seventy-five. What is it in London?'

'I don't know, Carl,' I'd say. He wasn't interested in the weather.

'I know. I got it right here on my phone: fifty-eight degrees. Fifty-eight. It's pathetic. And still you don't want to do Pilot Season.'

'Listen, Carl, the thing is . . .'

'I know, I know,' he'd say in a conciliatory tone, 'you told me, I get it. You don't want to come live here. The kids, your work, blah, blah. I get it. But if you made a pilot show here – one show – and it got picked up, you know what you'd be earning?'

'It's not about the money . . .'

'You'd have to work a year in the UK for what you'd get for a couple of episodes. A year.'

'I heard you, Carl.'

'And we have schools here, you know.'

'I know that. Look, it's just . . .'

'I get it.'

'My life's here.'

'I get it.'

'And the kids are happy and settled . . .'

'I get it. It's OK. You don't have to say any more. You don't want to make great money and spend every weekend walking barefoot with your husband by the ocean. I get it.

But at least come and take a couple of meetings. There was a part in a movie that came up last week. A snobby English nanny who turns out to be a down-at-heel duchess with a heart of gold. It was perfect for you . . .'

Eventually, Carl wore me down by sheer force of personality, and figuring I had nothing to lose but the price of a plane ticket, I went to LA. Carl promised to fix me up with a couple of what were known as 'Generals'. These were not specific auditions for an actual job; more a chance for a casting director to put a face to a name. I didn't expect them to know who I was from the work I'd done in Britain, but I did point out to Carl that a glance at my showreel or even a programme I'd been in would have saved me an eleven-hour commute. But these people, he explained, being bombarded day in and day out with showreels and faces and names, needed to put all three together before anything was likely to come of it, and I could see the logic in that. Besides it might be fun to meet casting directors working on long-running TV shows and blockbuster movies, and to look around those iconic studio lots I'd heard about in a thousand film-star anecdotes.

The same people who'd told me I'd love LA had also told me driving was a breeze. 'It's a city built for cars,' they all said. But one attempt at the wheel of a left-hand-drive car on what felt decidedly like the 'wrong side' of a freeway, and I knew this wasn't for me. So here I was in the back of a cab, heading to my first meeting. At Universal City. Gate 5. In half an hour's time.

I saw a sign for UCLA, and my driver flipped on his indicator and pulled into the exit lane.

'Oh God,' I said under my breath. And then out loud: 'I'm sorry, but it's NOT the university that I want.'

'I know that. Universal. With the rides and everything.'

'Yes. Well not the part with the rides, but we'll worry about that later. The main thing is, not here. Not to the university.'

'It's OK. It's OK. I just gotta pick up the share.'

I didn't know what that meant, but I seemed to have got my message across about Universal, so I wiped the sweat from the back of my neck and looked out of the window.

We turned into a small residential street, and the driver slowed to a crawl.

'3801, 3803 . . .' he was muttering to himself.

'Sorry, er . . . what are you looking for?'

'3805. Got it. Two minutes, lady,' he said.

He pulled up by the kerb and we sat with the engine ticking over. I was so completely bewildered by now that I couldn't even begin to frame my thoughts into a question. This was all my fault. It had to be. Maybe I'd got the booking wrong. Perhaps when I'd typed in 'Gate 5 Universal Studios' my phone had autocorrected it to '3805 Anonymous Little Side Street'. Maybe this wasn't a cab ride at all but an unusually benign and ineffectual kidnapping. The only thing I was sure of was that 3805 Nowhere Avenue wasn't where my bigshot casting director was going to be waiting. Frankly, the university would be preferable to this.

'Listen, I think there's been a misunderstanding,' I began. But before I could explain, the passenger door opened and a smart young guy got in.

'Hi,' he said to the driver. 'You got the address?'

'I got it. Cahuenga Boulevard. No problem. I'll get

you there in no time, and then I'll take this lady to the university.'

'Universal City,' I said, a little too aggressively.

'Wow,' said the new guy. 'You're in for a long ride.'

Then he buckled up his seat belt, took out his laptop, and started to answer emails.

I sat staring at the back of his head, performing a dumb show of incomprehension for nobody else but me. 'The nerve of this guy,' my dumb show attempted to convey, 'hijacking my taxi like it was the most natural thing in the world. Unbelievable!'

My phone rang. It was Carl.

'Progress?'

'Well, I'm running pretty late. I think you'll have to warn them.'

'Where are you now?' he asked.

'I'm not sure.'

'So ask your driver.'

'I'm not convinced we'll be any the wiser,' I muttered, 'but hang on.'

'Excuse me,' I called over the engine noise, 'whereabouts are we now?'

'Wilshire,' the driver answered.

'Wilshire,' I said into the phone.

'Wilshire?' Carl yelled. 'What the hell? Who goes via Wilshire? Put him on the phone.'

'He's driving the cab, Carl. We're on a busy road. I'd like to get there in one piece.'

'Then ask him WHY he's going via Wilshire.'

'I can't do that.'

'Why not?'

'Because I'm English and I don't *do* confrontation.'

'Try it for once in your life. Who's even gonna know?'

'The other passenger will for a start,' I hissed.

'What other passenger?' Carl barked. 'You got someone with you?'

I cupped my hand around the phone in an effort to stop his voice travelling to the front of the cab.

'He stopped and picked someone up. Like a hitch-hiker. He seemed to think it was no big deal.'

'Oh my God!' Carl yelled. 'You got a pool car?'

'I don't know. Did I?'

'You got a pool car. You share the ride and the fare. Didn't you see it on the screen when you booked?'

'I didn't even know there *was* such a thing.'

'OK, well there's no way you're gonna make it on time. I'll call ahead. Don't worry. Just tell your driver not to go on the 101.'

'OK,' I said.

'You're not gonna tell him, are you?'

'No,' I said.

At last Carl was beginning to understand me.

Time passed in a blur of unfamiliar place names. At least, they were all familiar from TV shows and the titles of films, but I had no idea how they related to one another geographically. I glanced ahead through the windscreen just in time to see a freeway sign. We were on the 101. Of course we were. It was that kind of a day.

There was nothing I could do about it now anyway, so I settled back into my seat and tried to visualise the meeting ahead with – what was her name again? Oh yes. Marcy

Kendall Kelly. She was a massively important casting director, according to Carl. Even taking into consideration his customary hyperbole, I could tell he was thrilled she was seeing me.

'This', he'd told me at least a dozen times, 'is a *significant* meeting.'

I'd be late, of course, but as long as Carl had rung ahead I could brush that aside with a brief apology and begin the process of selling myself. I had to be confident, that's what they liked over here. None of that self-deprecation crap. Straightforward, naked self-confidence.

I could do that; I just had to get into character.

'Hi, Kendall,' I'd begin. 'Good of you to find the time to meet me.'

Or meet 'with'? Maybe I should throw that into the mix. A nice little Americanism to show that I wasn't all 'British English is best'. After all, American English is closer to the English of Shakespeare than the way we speak back home. I might say that too, to break the ice with Kelly.

Not Kelly, Kendall. Kendall Kelly Marcy. Or was it Marcy Kelly Kendall? Yes, it was. I was sure of it. Kendall Marcy Kelly.

'Hi, Kendall,' I'd begin. 'Thank you for taking the time to meet with . . .'

Damn, was it Marcy Kelly Kendall or Kelly Kendall Marcy? I checked the calendar entry on my phone. It said: 'Meeting at Universal, 3.30 p.m. Gate 5. Not the one the tourists go to.'

How could I have forgotten to write her name?

I dialled Carl's number.

'How's Wilshire?' he yelled.

'We're not there any more,' I said.

'You're on the 101, aren't you?'

I hesitated.

'I knew it. Is it moving?'

'Yes it is,' I said defensively, and as I did, the driver slammed on the brakes so sharply that the guy in the passenger seat actually raised his eyes from his laptop.

'Doesn't look good. Hope you're not in a hurry,' he murmured over his shoulder, and went back to checking his emails.

'So, I've called ahead, and they're totally cool. Don't worry at all. She has another meeting at four thirty, so as long as you're there by four fifteen, you're gonna be fine.'

'That's great,' I said. I looked at my watch. It was three forty-five and ahead of me was a sea of tail lights. Another Americanism. Maybe I could throw that one in as well.

'Listen, Carl. Remind me of this woman's name again. I can't believe I didn't write it down.'

'I can't believe it either, but I also can't believe you got a pool car. OK. It's Marcy Kendall Kelly.'

'Of course it is,' I said, rummaging around for a pen and a piece of paper. 'What's the deal with you people and triple names? Two names aren't enough for you?'

'I just checked the traffic,' said Carl smugly. 'The 101's gridlocked, isn't it?'

I didn't want to give him the satisfaction.

'And surnames as first names,' I continued, 'that's something else I can't get my head around.'

'I'll call them again; tell them you're gonna be even later than I thought,' he said, and hung up.

I couldn't find a pen, so I opened the notepad app on my

phone. Marcy Kelly . . . Kendall Marcy . . . Kendall Kelly . . .? Damn. I couldn't face telling Carl I'd forgotten it already. I'd ask when I got to reception. *If* I got to reception.

Once we'd dropped off the cab-share guy in Cahuenga Boulevard, the pace started to pick up. So much so that I actually began to hope I might make this meeting after all. I could see road signs to Universal City, and when we approached the exit the driver began indicating before I even had a chance to yell at him.

'OK,' he said triumphantly as we turned off the road. 'Universal Studios. I told you I'd get you here.'

'Great,' I said. 'Thank you. So, is this Gate 5?'

'Universal Studios. It said on the sign.'

'I know, but is it Gate 5?'

'It's Universal Studios,' he said with a hint of irritation. 'That's where you want to go, right?'

We were driving towards a security gate, and he wound down his window.

'I got a lady for the studio,' he said to the guard.

'May I see your ticket, please?'

I wound my window down too.

'Sorry, what ticket?'

'For the studio tour. I need to check your ticket, ma'am.'

'I'm not here for the studio tour,' I said, trying to suppress the note of panic in my voice. 'I'm here for the studios. Universal Studios.'

'That's right, ma'am.'

'I have a meeting. With a casting director. Called Kendall . . . Kelly . . . it's in the casting department.'

'Oh you want to be at Gate 5, ma'am,' said the guard.

'OK,' I sighed. 'So, could you tell us how we get there, please?'

'No problem. You go out of here and make a right at the gas station, then first left, second right and straight on for about five hundred feet and you'll see it.'

'That's terrific,' I said, and we started to pull away.

'So you got all that, did you?' I asked the driver.

'Got what, lady?' he replied.

'OK, could you back up, please?'

He jammed the cab into reverse and I saw the security guard jump out of the way. I wound my window down again.

'I'm so sorry, could you repeat all of that so my driver gets it.'

'Sure, no problem. You go out of here –'

'Wait a minute,' I interrupted. The driver was tapping something into his onboard computer. I suspected it was the details of his next fare.

'Are you listening? Because this where I need you to take me to and it's very important.'

He stopped what he was doing. I think he'd picked up on the hysterical pitch of my voice.

'Sure thing. I'll take you anywhere you wanna go.'

'Great,' I said, before turning back to the guard. 'I'm sorry. Go ahead.'

Gate 5, when we finally got there some twelve minutes later, was kind of hard to miss. The enormous sign saying 'GATE 5' above the barriers was a sure-fire clue. Even so, my driver almost overshot it.

'It's this one!' I yelled into his ear.

'This one?' he said, as if I must have divined this by some strange magic. 'You sure?'

'Yes,' I said. 'Gate 5. Can you see? There's a big sign above it.'

'Gate 5, yes. I got it. I said I was gonna get you there.'

I got out of the car, and was immediately hit by the over-powering, mid-afternoon Californian heat. I could actually feel my make-up sliding off my face.

I walked up to the security gate and said I was here for a meeting in the casting department.

'Do you have the name of the person you're going to see, ma'am?'

I hesitated, then thought that maybe if I just took a run at it, it might come out in the right order.

'Kendall Kelly Marcy,' I rattled off. The guard looked at his clipboard. He turned over a page. Then another.

'I don't think we have anyone here by that name,' he frowned.

'Might it be down under my name, do you think?'

He carefully scanned the list as the last of my mascara dripped on to my cheek.

'There you are,' he suddenly announced. 'I got you. OK, here's your pass. You need to go to Building 405. Right down to the end there and take a left. You can't miss it.'

I thanked him profusely, and started to run. It must have been 90 degrees out; I could have killed Carl and his 'balmy seventy-five'. As I jogged down the main pathway, I could hear from behind me one of the tour buses being driven around the lot.

'Now if you look over to your right, folks,' a quirky, chirpy pre-recorded voice was saying, 'you might recognise that little fella standing outside Building 251.' I looked across as well, and saw a large plastic statue of a cartoon animal in front of an anonymous office block.

'That's right,' the voice-over chuckled, 'it's Marshall Moose, star of 879 cartoon shows back in the early seventies. Each and every one of those shows was scripted right here in Building 251.'

The people on the tour bus all lifted their phones and took photos of Marshall Moose and the dull, grey, breeze-block cradle of his creation.

I carried on scuttling down the road. The bus was closer to me now.

'And if you glance up at the trees to the left of Marshall Moose,' the voice was saying, 'you're gonna see another old friend.'

The tour group craned their necks, then turned to each other and nodded knowingly.

'You got it,' cried the voice-over, with a hearty laugh. 'It's his old adversary Vulture Vic. Hold on to your valuables, folks, cos nothing's safe if Vulch is around.'

I'd found it. Building 405. I couldn't see anything resembling a main entrance though. I tried a couple of fire doors at the front, but they were all locked. So I walked round to the side. The doors were locked there too. I carried on round to the next side. Then the next and the next, which was of course the front again. How the hell was I supposed to get inside?

By now, my clothes and hair were sticking to me. The pale pink pumps I'd put on for the first time that day were grey with gravel dust. I tried the first door again and when it still didn't budge, I stood looking at the building, shaking my head in despair.

'Now over here on your left', I imagined the tour guide was saying, 'is a crazy, sweating British actress. You may have seen her in a couple of shows back in her own country, but frankly (hearty chuckle), she's wasting her time and money coming over here. Take a good look at her, folks. (Guffaw.) Boy, has she ever messed this up!'

I turned around disconsolately and began heading back towards the entrance. I might as well walk the seven miles to my hotel; it couldn't take me any longer than the cab ride here. And it would give me time to think of what to say to Carl.

I saw a young man walking towards me wheeling an empty porter's trolley. He smiled at me, and he had such an open face that I thought it might be worth one final shot.

'Excuse me, you don't happen to know how I get into Building 405, do you?'

'Well, I know where the packages go in. It's not, like, a lobby or anything, but I can get you to a staircase, if that'll help.'

'Could you? I'd be so grateful.'

He looked me up and down for a moment, and something clearly told him I was close to the edge. He leant his trolley up against a wall and said, 'Wait right there.'

Seconds later he reappeared riding one of those electric golf buggies.

'Hop on,' he said.

As we rode around the building in peaceful, battery-powered comfort, I suddenly realised for the first time that this was a pretty incredible moment. Here I was, an English actress, being driven around a Hollywood studio on my way to a meeting with a casting director. How many times had I imagined this when I was a child? Admittedly, in my dreams I would have been smartly dressed and significantly less sweaty, but nonetheless, no one could take this away from me.

The golf buggy pulled up at a gigantic warehouse entrance. I'd seen it earlier, but it was clearly locked. There was a little door to the side of it though, tucked into an alcove, which my guardian angel tried, and it opened.

'Just go through to the end and make a left along the corridor. There's elevators and stairs there and that should take you where you want to go,' he said.

I actually wanted to kiss him, but I settled instead for a firm handshake. And before I knew it, a line worthy of the hokiest Hollywood movie had come out of my mouth.

'Those people doing the tours,' I said, 'they've come all this way to get a glimpse of a studio. But I got to meet an actual star.'

He gave an embarrassed shrug, hopped back on the golf cart and drove away.

I followed his instructions past the mail room and a maintenance office. There were signs for ventilation shafts and dry riser outlets, but no mention of the casting department. At last, I found the staircase, legged it up a couple of flights, stopped briefly at the top to mop my face with a tissue, and walked purposefully to the reception desk.

'May I help you?'

'Yes,' I said. 'I have a meeting with Kendall . . . with Kelly . . . I have a casting meeting. My name's Rebecca Front.'

'No problem,' said the receptionist. 'Marcy's on a call. Take a seat.'

I sat on a couch and tried to compose myself, blowing my damp fringe out of my eyes and tugging at my clothes where they'd stuck to my body.

'So,' said the receptionist, looking at me quizzically, '. . . have you had far to come today?'

ACKNOWLEDGEMENTS

Thanks to my agent Charlie Campbell, for believing that I could write books and not letting me off the hook until I'd done so. Also to my editor Alan Samson and erstwhile editor Bea Hemming, to Julia Kingsford, Simon Wright and everyone at Orion for their encouragement and support. But mostly, thanks to my wonderful parents, my incredible children, my endlessly supportive husband and all my family and friends for allowing me to plunder our lives together for material.